W9-BJC-597

Mes Confitures

Mes Confitures

The Jams and Jellies of Christine Ferber

CHRISTINE FERBER

Translated by Virginia R. Phillips

Michigan State University Press · *East Lansing*

∞ The paper used in this publication meets the minimum requirements
of ANSI/NISO Z39.48-1992 (R 1997) (Permanence of Paper).

Michigan State University Press
East Lansing, Michigan 48823-5245

Printed and bound in China.

08 07 06 05 04 03 02   1 2 3 4 5 6 7 8 9 10

LIBRARY OF CONGRESS CATALOGING-IN-PUBLICATION DATA
Ferber, Christine.
[Mes confitures. English]
Mes confitures : the jams and jellies of Christine Ferber /
Christine Ferber ; translated by Virginia R. Phillips.
p. cm.
Includes index.
ISBN 0-87013-629-1 (cloth : alk. paper)
1. Jelly. I. Title.
TX612.J4 F47 2002
641.8'52—dc21
2002001565

Cover design by Ariana Grabec-Dingman
Book design by Sharp Des!gns, Inc., Lansing, MI

My Jams and Jellies
In creative collaboration with Gilles and Laurence Laurendon
Photos: Berhard Winkelmann
The photos in this book were taken at the *Ecomusée at Ungersheim.*
My gratitude to François-Xavier Streicher and Philippe Donato for the lovely objects they let me borrow.
© 1997, Éditions Payot & Rivages, 2000, Editions Payot & Rivages for the revised French edition.
106 Blvd. Saint-Germain, Paris VIᵉ

Visit Michigan State University Press on the World Wide Web at *www.msupress.msu.edu*

To Fréderick and Pierre Hermé.

To my family.

Contents

Foreword

1960: The story begins in France, in Alsace, an area next to the Swiss and German borders, in the little village of Niedermorschwihr. Christine Ferber, daughter of fourth-generation bakers and pastry-makers, grew up to the rhythms of her parents' livelihood, nurtured by the bakery's glorious fragrances.

Even as a little girl Christine was inquisitive, and a connoisseur. She liked to spend hours watching her father work. She could feel her senses awakening one by one, as a spectator at this irresistible show. At age eleven under her father's loving and skillful eye she tried her hand at pastry-making. Those memories remain very present for her today—the Saturday/Sunday blend of sweet and savory, the flavors and aromas of quetsch plum tarts, kugelhopfs, terrines and pâtés baked in pastry.

Having become an apprentice without quite choosing to be, Christine was soon confronted by the tough reality of the professional baker's world. The shy youngster's hard and not very gratifying assignment was cleaning her father's workplace. Then, because Alsatian pastry masters refused to teach the profession to a woman, she took her parents' advice and left home to spend three years in Brussels, Belgium.

She returned to her family an impassioned and determined young professional, her head full of plans and memories. She could still taste the fruit treasures she had encountered in her gourmet escapades. She couldn't get the sweetness of her grandmother's preserves out of her head. One summer day she decided to recapture the flavors, colors, and melodic sounds of her childhood. She selected a copper pan and made her first sour cherry preserves. A few jars would be the perfect decorative touch in the window of the family's grocery store. She'd never dreamed they might sell. And yet . . .

Today, recognized by her peers, she pursues her culinary adventures in time with the seasons and her own insatiable quest for flavors. Her jam in two hundred variations ravishes the taste buds of gastronomes in the four corners of the world.

Highly trained in pastry, jams and chocolate, Christine Ferber is a gentle and reserved person who gives expression to her emotions through creativity. People describe how she likes to dream up new recipes with her eyes shut. Not shut entirely, though: from her pastry school education she knows the importance of technique. Her secrets are precision and patience—precision in choosing and measuring ingredients and in cooking method and temperature; patience, so that the jam becomes an expression of sensuality and conviviality, a wonderful moment to share with people we love.

In Monaco in my gourmet restaurant, Le Louis XV, I serve her Alsatian Morello cherry preserves with L'Ossau-Iraty. The lightly caramelized fruit bring a touch of tartness and color to the Basque sheep cheese.

Christine's jams intensify all the best that nature has to offer. With each spoonful you feel as if you are sinking your teeth into just-picked fruit. You take in a flurry of little surprises—a floral note, a pinch of spice, a little citrus zest, a hint of alcohol.

Ripe tomatoes and apples with rosemary, yellow peaches with lavender honey. Figs with Gewürztraminer and pine nuts, strawberries with black pepper and fresh mint, melon with citrus zest and preserved ginger . . . My favorite? Every one of them. It makes no difference whether I'm having preserves on toast or just dipping my finger in the jar, I enjoy them all with the same voluptuous pleasure.

In this book, Christine Ferber shares her sensitivity and skill. With love, poetry and passion, she invites us to experience her palate, her culinary "palace," where the symphony of flavors transcends the magic of sugar.

Deliciously yours,

Alain Ducasse

Publisher's Note

Equivalents

Like much of the world, France uses metric measurements in cooking. These have been converted to English measure, with the original metric amounts in parentheses. In some recipes, a metric equivalent does not appear. The original French measurement was either a "knifepoint" or a "coffeespoon," for example. These measures have been converted into teaspoons. A "knifepoint" is about ⅛ of a teaspoon. Please see Sources for more information on conversion.

Sources

The elegance and deep flavors of Christine Ferber's jams, jellies, and preserves stem from the combination of sound culinary technique married with fresh, local fruits and a rich imagination. Ideally, readers who live and cook outside of Alsace will find Christine's recipes not only fascinating and delicious, but inspirational. Local farmers' markets, farm stands, wineries, and other producers are rich sources for the freshest ingredients. Home cooks are encouraged to use their imaginations and seek out the best local ingredients. Particular types of fruits or chocolates are referenced in individual recipes. The following companies and organizations are also good sources for hard-to-find and imported foodstuffs:

Specialty Items, Imported, and Gourmet Foods

- King Arthur Flour, Norwich, VT; tel 800/827-6836; *www.kingarthurflour.com*
- Zingermans, 422 Detroit Street, Ann Arbor, MI 48104; e-mail *toni@zingermans.com*; tel 877/665-3213 or 734/477-5711; fax 734/769-1260; *www.zingermans.com*
- Ethnic Grocer.com; *www.ethnicgrocer.com*
- Dean and Deluca, Attn: Customer Assistance, 2526 East 36th Street North Circle, Wichita, KS 67219; tel 877/826-9246; fax 800/781-4050. New York location: 800/999-0306 ext. 268; *atyourservice@deananddeluca.com*; *www.deananddeluca.com*
- Murray's Cheese Shop, 257 Bleecker Street, New York City, NY 10014; tel 888/692-4339 (MY CHEEZ); *www.murrayscheese.com*
- Earthy Delights, 1161 E. Clark Road, Suite 260, DeWitt, MI 48820; tel 800/367-4709 or 517/668-2402; fax 517/668-1213; *www.earthy.com*
- National Association of Specialty Food Trade Association; *www.specialty-food.com*
- A Southern Season; tel 800/253 3663; fax 800/646 1118; *www.southernseason.com*
- Harry and David; *www.harry-david.com*
- Sutton Place Gourmet, 3201 New Mexico Ave. NW, Washington, D.C. 20016; tel 202/363-5800; *www.suttongourmet.com*
- Zabar's, 2245 Broadway, New York, NY 10024; tel 800/697-6301; *www.zabars.com*
- Draeger's Gourmet Food and Wine, 222 E. Fourth Street, San Mateo, CA 94401; tel 650/685-3715; e-mail *info@dreagers.com*; *www.draegers.com*
- Cherry Marketing Institute; *www.cherrymkt.org*
- Specialty Produce Market; tel 619/295-1668; *www.specialtyproduce.com*
- Melissa's/World Variety Produce, Inc., Corporate Office, P.O. Box 21127, Los Angeles, CA 90021; tel 800/588-0151; e-mail *Hotline@melissas.com*; *www.melissas.com*
- Frieda's, The Specialty Produce People; *www.friedas.com*

- Sid Wainer & Sons, Specialty Produce, Specialty Foods, 2301 Purchase Street, New Bedford, MA 02746; tel 508/999-6408 or 800/423-8333; fax 508/999-6795; *www.sidwainer.com*
- VegiWorks, Inc.; *www.vegiworks.com*
- Indian River Groves; tel 800/940-3344; *www.floridafruit.com*
- Blackjack Orchards; tel 858/565-0684; fax 858/565-6440; *www.blackjackorchards.com*
- E-Berries, Solimar Farms, Inc., Oxnard, California; tel 877/4BERRIES (877/423-7743); fax 805/986-1178; e-mail *info@e-berries.com*; *www.e-berries.com*
- Pearson Farms Peaches and Pecans; tel 888/423-7374; *www.pearsonfarm.com*
- Diamond Organics; tel 888-ORGANIC (674-2642); fax 888/888-6777; *www.diamondorganics.com*
- Bouquet of Fruits, 2037 W. Bullard, Box 302, Fresno, CA 93711; tel 559/432-9135 or 800/243-7848; fax 559/432-7509; *www.californiatreeripe.com*

For Chocolate
- *www.chocosphere.com*

Teas and Spices
- Seattle Spice, Herbs, and Tea, World Spice Merchants, 1509 Western Avenue, Seattle, WA 98101; tel 206/682-7274; fax 206/622-7564; *www.worldspice.com*
- Penzey's Spice World; tel 800/741-7787; fax 262/785-7678; *www.penzeys.com*

Books and Other Resources
- "The Splendid Table," with Lynne Rossetto Kasper; Minnesota Public Radio; *www.splendidtable.com*
- Home canning techniques and equipment; *www.homecanning.com*
- *Ball Blue Book*, Alltrista Corporation. A classic source for canning technique and safety, from the Ball Company.

- *Food Finds: America's Best Local Foods and the People Who Produce Them*, Allison Engel and Margaret Engel. HarperCollins, New York
- *The Joy of Cooking*, Irma S. Rombauer and Marion Rombauer Becker. MacMillan, New York
- *http://www.onlineconversion.com/cooking.htm*
- *www.globalgourmet.com*

Fairy Godmother of *Jams & Jellies*

All knowledgeable food lovers in France have heard of Christine Ferber, the "fairy godmother of jams and jellies." This young master pastry and dessert chef lives and works in Niedermorschwihr, the small Alsatian village where she was born. Her jams and jellies and sweet-sour confections have won over the biggest-name chefs—Alain Ducasse, the Troisgros family, and Antoine Westermann, among them—and have earned a reputation today in Germany, Belgium, and Japan.

Christine is an artist and an impassioned one. She personally selects the fruit for her jams from local farmers. Mulberries, wild raspberries, or rose hips may come from baskets brought to her by people out for a walk. Wild apples, acacia blossoms, and rose petals she picks herself. She uses only seasonal fruit and makes her jams in small batches—never more than eight pounds at a time.

This virtuoso of flavors has offered us her recipe notebook: Morello cherry jam, apple with fresh mint . . . apple with acacia flower jelly, black cherry with Pinot Noir, chestnut and walnut . . . She's added her latest creations as well: quince, orange, and cardamom jam and New Year's jam.

Whether the recipes are traditional or daring, they are explained simply and will be a delight to anyone who loves sweets.

Genius amounts to nothing more than a lot of patience!

Gilles & Laurence Laurendon

Techniques & Ingredients

Jam-making, too, is the school of patience.

JEAN-PIERRE COFFE

The Fruit

Most of the fruit I use is picked in Alsatian orchards or woods. It is gathered either in the morning, after the dew has evaporated and before the sun becomes too hot, or toward the end of the afternoon. Fruit picked in hot sun or in the rain never makes good jam. Rain makes the fruit soggy; heat exaggerates the fragrance and makes the fruit soft.

Fruit is perfectly ripe when it makes no resistance to being picked. This is the point at which it presents a good balance in acidity and pectin, which helps the jam to set. I always use fresh, very fragrant, healthy fruit with no bruising whatever. It doesn't matter whether fruit is picked in the woods, a garden, or orchard or bought from growers or at a market, there's only one rule: it should look beautiful and have wonderful flavor.

Ideally, the fruit should be prepared a few hours after picking—the next day at the latest (and, if so, the fruit must be kept cool)—because it loses quality quickly. My preference is to cook it in small quantities. I never put more than eight pounds of fruit in a pan: small batches preserve the natural color and texture of the fruit.

When I'm macerating or cooking fruit, I always use fresh lemon juice. The fruit, sugar, and lemon juice should be combined quickly to prevent oxidization of the fruit and to preserve its color. The lemon's touch of acidity brings out the fruit's flavor and activates the gelling power of its pectin. I pour macerated and cooked preparations into ceramic bowls and cover them with parchment paper so that fruit is immersed in the syrup and doesn't darken on the surface.

Sugar & Cooking

Jam making is essentially preserving fruit with sugar. For the best preservation effect, the jam should be sixty-five percent sugar. If we know that fruit normally has ten to fifteen percent sugar, we add sugar to each batch approximately equivalent to the weight of the fruit. If riper fruit is being used, the amount of sugar is reduced. I always use sparkling white, good-quality sugar. Quite often, I'll macerate the fruit and then cook it several times. I do this so that the sugar is absorbed gradually by the fruit, and the texture of the fruit is preserved.

With some recipes, you stop the fruit from cooking further by immersing it in a syrup. The syrup is a mixture of sugar and the macerating juice, which has been reduced to a greater or lesser extent by boiling. You may wish to monitor the degree of concentration with a thermometer. This technique is a variation that preserves the fruit's texture.

Apple jelly supplies pectin, an essential to the gelling process for fruits that don't have it naturally, such as pears, sour cherries, and Morello cherries. You can get the same results with longer cooking. But your jam will be sweeter, the fruit will have a little less attractive texture, and the color will be caramelized.

To achieve perfect consistency, I advise you to check the set. Jam has to reach 221°F [105°C] on a candy thermometer. If you don't have a thermometer, put a few drops of jam on a cold plate and check the consistency. With a little practice, you won't need these tests. You will be able to tell at a glance the minute that the jam has finished cooking and is ready to be put into the jars. You'll see that the evaporation is noticeably decreasing, that there is no longer any foam on the surface, that the fruit is submerged in the syrup, and that the bubbles are disappearing.

What I'm explaining to you here is my way of doing it. With time and practice, you will refine your own technique. And before long you'll bring your imagination into play and put together some unexpected flavors. Remind yourself that no two jams are ever the same. From one year to another, one batch to another, a little thinner, a little thicker, each is different—this is what gives them their charm.

A batch of jam is always an act of creation!

Equipment

I always use a copper preserving pan because it guarantees excellent heat distribution for cooking. This type of pan is wider than it is deep, which lets the liquid from the fruit evaporate better. It shouldn't be used for anything but jam making. Never use a copper pan for macerating fruit. The fruit will oxidize.

You can also use a large, nonreactive pot, such as a stockpot, but the fruit will have a tendency to stick on the bottom. You'll have to be even more vigilant.

The skimmer is stainless steel. It's used to skim, of course, but also for gently stirring the jam, checking how the syrup is cooking, removing spices from the pan, and when some preparations are finished, for lifting out fruit that will be put into the jars.

I have a wooden spoon that I use only for making jam.

I use a stainless steel ladle for filling the jars.

A stainless zester and a paring knife are essentials for preparing fruit.

Also necessary:
- a cutting board
- a standing colander for rinsing and draining the fruit
- a food mill, with a set of disks, for removing seeds and skin in some preparations
- a nonreactive metal pan for blanching fruit zest
- a lid that fits the preserving pan

- two ceramic bowls for peeled fruit, for collecting juice for the jellies, for cooking syrups, and for macerating some preparations before cooking
- a kitchen scale to weigh the ingredients
- a fine-mesh, conical sieve, called a *chinois*, and a piece of muslin or cheesecloth to filter the juice for jellies
- a wide sieve to drain the fruit after a preliminary cooking
- a piece of muslin or cheesecloth to make a bag to hold seeds or pits
- a mixer
- a lemon squeezer or reamer
- a zester
- a nutcracker
- parchment paper to cover your preparations
- two kitchen towels
- a candy thermometer, graduated to 400°F [200°C]
- a jam funnel for filling jars more easily
- canning jars
- new, screw-on lids
- labels

Filling the Jars & Storing the Jam

I use standard, faceted glass jars. The jars should be in perfect, unchipped condition. They should close very simply with a screw top. In the United States, Ball makes jars with two-part, sealing screw-top lids.

Before making jam, I sterilize the jars, either by putting them in boiling water for a few minutes or by putting them in a 225°F [108°C] oven for 5 minutes.

As soon as the jam has finished cooking, I fill the jars, using the small ladle and the jam funnel. I fill them right up to the top. Any drips should be carefully wiped off. I close the jars while they are hot and turn them upside down.

I wait until they are cool to put the labels on and then put the jars in a cool, dry place, out of the light.

Spring

Spring Carrot with Cinnamon

Scant 3 pounds [1.3 kg] carrots, *or* 2¼ pounds [1 kg] net
2 cups plus 1 ounce [500 g/50 cl] water
3¾ cups [800 g] granulated sugar
Juice of 1 small lemon
1 cinnamon stick

Wash the carrots and peel them, carefully removing any green parts of the core, which are hard and bitter.

Grate the carrots on a fine grater. Stir the carrots into the water in a preserving pan. Bring to a boil and cook on low heat for about 20 minutes, stirring occasionally. After 20 minutes, there will be no more water in the pan, and the carrots will be soft.

Add the sugar, cinnamon stick, and lemon juice. Bring it to a boil again, stirring gently. Continue cooking for 10 minutes, stirring continuously. Skim if necessary. Remove the cinnamon stick, which you can use to decorate the jars. Bring to a boil again. Check the set. Put the jam in jars immediately and seal.

Carrot, Orange, and Cardamom

Scant 3 pounds [1.3 kg] carrots, *or* 2¼ pounds [1 kg] net
4⅔ cups [1 kg] granulated sugar
7 ounces [250 g/25 cl] orange juice
Juice of 1 small lemon
2½ teaspoons [5 g] ground cardamom
⅜ teaspoon finely grated orange zest

Wash the carrots and peel them, carefully removing any green parts in the core, which are hard and bitter.

Grate the carrots on a fine grater. Combine the carrots, sugar, orange zest, orange juice, lemon juice, and cardamom in a preserving pan. Bring to a simmer. Pour into a ceramic bowl. Cover with a sheet of parchment paper and refrigerate overnight.

Next day, bring this mixture to a boil. Skim and cook on high heat for about 10 minutes, stirring gently. Check the set. Put the jam in jars immediately and seal.

~:~

The carrot/cardamom combination was inspired by a delicious Indian dessert. The carrots in the "Carrot, Orange, and Cardamom" recipe maintain the texture of partly cooked vegetables, whereas in the "Carrot and Cinnamon" recipe, the texture will be a purée.

White Cherry with Raspberry

2¾ pounds [1.25 kg] white Napoleon cherries, *or* 2¼ pounds [1 kg] net

9 ounces (*about 2 cups*) [250 g] raspberries

3 tablespoons [50 g/5 cl] water

4⅓ cups [950 g] granulated sugar

Juice of 1 lemon

7 ounces [200 g] Green Apple Jelly (*page 120*)

Rinse the cherries in cold water and dry them in a towel. Stem and pit them. Combine them in a ceramic bowl with the sugar and lemon juice. After an hour of maceration, pour the mixture into a preserving pan and bring it to a simmer. Pour into a ceramic bowl. Cover the fruit with a sheet of parchment paper and refrigerate overnight.

Next day, bring the raspberries and the water to a boil in a covered saucepan and let the fruit soften on low heat for 5 minutes. Collect the juice by pouring the mixture through a chinois sieve; then, filter it through cheesecloth.

Put the white cherry preparation into a sieve. Pour the collected juice into a preserving pan. Add the apple jelly and raspberry juice; bring the juices to a boil and cook for about 5 minutes. Skim carefully. Add the cherries. Bring to a boil again and continue cooking on high heat for about 5 minutes, stirring gently. Skim again if needed. Check the set. Put the jam in jars immediately and seal.

White Cherry à la Rose

2¾ pounds [1.25 kg] white Napoleon cherries, *or* 2¼ pounds [1 kg] net
4¼ cups [900 g] granulated sugar
Juice of 1 small lemon
7 ounces [200 g] Green Apple Jelly (*page 120*)
1 teaspoon [100 drops/5 cl] rose water
2 handfuls of untreated, dried rose petals

Rinse the cherries in cold water and dry them in a towel. Stem and pit them. Combine them in a ceramic bowl with the sugar and lemon juice. After an hour of maceration, pour this mixture into a preserving pan and bring to a simmer. Pour into a ceramic bowl. Cover the fruit with a sheet of parchment paper and refrigerate overnight.

Next day, put the white cherry preparation into a sieve. Pour the collected juice into a preserving pan. Add the apple jelly, bring to a boil, and cook for 5 minutes. Skim carefully. Add the cherries. Return to a boil and continue cooking on high heat for about 5 minutes, stirring gently. Skim again, if need be. Check the set. Add the rose water and rose petals. Put the jam in jars immediately and seal.

Black Cherry and Raspberry with Kirsch

2¾ pounds [1.25 kg] black cherries, *or* 2¼ pounds [1 kg] net
9 ounces (*about 2½ cups*) [250 g] raspberries
4⅔ cups [1 kg] granulated sugar
Juice of 1 small lemon
7 ounces [200 g] Green Apple Jelly (*page 120*)
1 ounce [30 g/3 cl] kirsch

Rinse the cherries in cold water and dry them in a towel. Stem and pit them. Combine them in a ceramic bowl with the sugar and lemon juice. After an hour of maceration, pour into a preserving pan and bring to a simmer. Pour into a ceramic bowl. Cover the mixture with a sheet of parchment paper and refrigerate overnight.

Next day, put the raspberries through a food mill (fine disk).

Pour the black cherry preparation into a sieve. Pour the collected juice into a preserving pan. Add the apple jelly and raspberry pulp. Boil for 5 minutes. Skim carefully. Now add the black cherries. Return to a boil again and continue cooking on high heat for 5 minutes, stirring gently. Skim again if necessary. Check the set. Add the kirsch. Put the jam in jars immediately and seal.

Black Cherry

2¾ pounds [1.25 kg] black cherries, *or* 2¼ pounds [1 kg] net
3¾ cups [800 g] granulated sugar
Juice of 1 small lemon
7 ounces [200 g] Green Apple Jelly (*page 120*)

Rinse the cherries in cold water and dry them in a towel. Stem and pit them. Combine them with the sugar and lemon juice in a ceramic bowl. After an hour of maceration, pour into a preserving pan and bring to a simmer. Pour into a ceramic bowl. Cover with a sheet of parchment paper and refrigerate overnight.

Next day, put the preparation into a sieve. Pour the collected juice into a preserving pan. Add the apple jelly, bring to a boil, and boil 5 minutes. Skim carefully. Add the cherries. Return to a boil and continue cooking for about 5 minutes, stirring gently. Skim again, if need be. Check the set. Put the jam in jars immediately and seal.

Black Cherry with Pinot Noir

2¾ pounds [1.25 kg] black cherries, *or* 2¼ pounds [1 kg] net
4¼ cups [900 g] granulated sugar
Juice of 1 small lemon
7 ounces [200 g] Green Apple Jelly (*page 120*)
8½ ounces [250 g/25 cl] Pinot Noir

Rinse the cherries in cold water and dry them in a towel. Stem and pit them. Combine them in a ceramic bowl with the sugar and lemon juice. After an hour of maceration, pour into a preserving pan and bring to a simmer. Pour into a ceramic bowl. Cover the fruit with a sheet of parchment paper and refrigerate overnight.

Next day, put the preparation into a sieve. Pour the collected juice into a preserving pan. Add the apple jelly, bring to a boil, and boil for 5 minutes. Add the Pinot Noir and continue boiling 5 minutes more. Skim carefully. Now add the black cherries. Return to a boil and continue cooking on high heat for about 5 minutes, stirring gently. Skim again if need be. Check the set. Put the jam into jars immediately and seal.

~:~

The Pinot Noir selected for this recipe is a low-tannin wine with flavors of red fruits, both wild and orchard grown. Pinot Noir with these characteristics can be used to enhance jams made with raspberries, Morello cherries, or blueberries.

Black Cherry with Eucalyptus Honey and Fresh Mint

2¾ pounds [1.25 kg] black cherries, *or* 2¼ pounds [1 kg] net
2¾ cups [600 g] granulated sugar
7 ounces [200 g] eucalyptus honey
Juice of 1 small lemon
10 fresh mint leaves
7 ounces [200 g] Green Apple Jelly (*page 120*)

Rinse the cherries in cold water and dry them in a towel. Stem and pit them. Combine them in a ceramic bowl with the sugar, honey, and lemon juice. After an hour of maceration, pour into a preserving pan and bring to a simmer. Pour into a ceramic bowl. Cover the fruit with a sheet of parchment paper and refrigerate overnight.

Next day, put the preparation into a sieve. Pour the collected juice into a preserving pan. Add the apple jelly, bring to a boil, and boil 5 minutes. Skim carefully. Now add the cherries. Return to a boil again and continue cooking on high heat for about 5 minutes, stirring gently. Add the mint leaves and return to a boil. Skim again, if needed. Check the set. Put the jam into jars immediately and seal.

*Morello Cherry**

2¾ pounds [1.25 kg] Morello cherries, *or* 2¼ pounds [1 kg] net
3¾ cups [800 g] granulated sugar
Juice of 1 small lemon
7 ounces [200 g] **Green Apple Jelly** (*page 120*)

Rinse the cherries in cold water and dry them in a towel. Stem and pit them. Combine them in a ceramic bowl with the sugar and lemon juice. After an hour of maceration, pour into a preserving pan and bring to a simmer. Pour into a ceramic bowl. Cover the fruit with a sheet of parchment paper and refrigerate overnight.

Next day, put the preparation into a sieve. Pour the collected juice into a preserving pan. Add the apple jelly, bring to a boil, and boil 5 minutes. Skim carefully. Now add the cherries. Bring to a boil once more and continue cooking on high heat for about 5 minutes, stirring gently. Skim again, if needed. Check the set. Put the jam into jars immediately and seal.

~:~

I particularly like Morello cherries for their tartness. This classic Morello cherry jam is also the first jam I ever made. The small Morellos have a pronounced almond taste that goes perfectly with little sugar cookies or Genoa bread.† Try some of the jam on almond-milk ice cream.

---

* *The Morello is a sour, dark cherry. In the United States, the Balaton cherry is a Morello varietal available in Michigan, a major cherry-producing state. Tart "pie" cherries may also be used. See Sources, page xi.*
† *Genoa bread is a cake flavored with butter and almonds.*

Morello Cherry with Almond*

2¾ pounds [1.25 kg] Morello cherries, or 2¼ pounds [1 kg] net

3¾ cups [800 g] granulated sugar

Juice of 1 small lemon

7 ounces [200 g] Green Apple Jelly (*page 120*)

1¾ cups [150 g] slivered almonds

Rinse the cherries in cold water and dry them in a towel. Stem and pit them. Save the pits, crush them, and tie them in a cheesecloth bag.

Combine the cherries in a ceramic bowl with the sugar and lemon juice. After an hour of maceration, pour into a preserving pan with the muslin bag holding the pits and bring to a simmer. Pour into a ceramic bowl. Cover the fruit with a sheet of parchment paper and refrigerate overnight.

Next day, put the preparation into a sieve. Pour the collected juice into a preserving pan. Add the apple jelly, bring to a boil, and boil 5 minutes. Skim carefully. Add the cherries. Return to a boil and continue cooking on high heat for about 5 minutes, stirring gently. Add the slivered almonds and return to a boil. Skim again, if needed. Remove the bag of cherry pits. Check the set. Put the jam into jars immediately and seal.

* The Morello is a sour, dark cherry. In the United States, the Balaton cherry is a Morello varietal available in Michigan, a major cherry-producing state. Tart "pie" cherries may also be used. See Sources, page xi.

Morello Cherry and Apple with Fresh Mint*

2¾ pounds [1.25 kg] Morello cherries, *or* 2¼ pounds [1 kg] net
3¾ cups [800 g] granulated sugar *plus* 2¼ cups [500 g]
1¾ pounds [800 g] Ida Red apples†, *or* 1¼ pounds [600 g] net
Juice of 1 small lemon
10 leaves fresh mint

Rinse the cherries in cold water and dry them in a towel. Stem and pit them. Combine them in a ceramic bowl with 3¾ cups [800 g] sugar and the lemon juice. After an hour of maceration, pour into a preserving pan and bring to a simmer. Pour into a ceramic bowl. Cover the fruit with a sheet of parchment paper and refrigerate overnight.

Next day, put the preparation into a sieve. Pour the collected juice into a preserving pan. Bring to a boil and boil 5 minutes. Meanwhile, peel the apples, remove the stems and cores, halve them, and cut them into thin slices. Put the apple slices and 2¼ cups [450 g] sugar into the pan. Continue cooking on high heat, stirring constantly for 5 minutes. Skim carefully. Add the cherries. Return to a boil and continue cooking on high heat for about 5 minutes, stirring gently. Add the mint leaves and return to a boil. Skim again, if need be. Check the set. Put the jam into jars immediately and seal.

* The Morello is a sour, dark cherry. In the United States, the Balaton cherry is a Morello varietal available in Michigan, a major cherry-producing state. Tart "pie" cherries may also be used. See Sources, page xi.
† Ida Red apples are large, bright red apples with firm, crisp, and slightly acidic white flesh.

*Morello Cherry with Rose Petals**

2¾ pounds [1.25 kg] Morello cherries, *or* 2¼ pounds [1 kg] net
3¾ cups [800 g] granulated sugar
Juice of 1 small lemon
7 ounces [200 g] Green Apple Jelly (*page 120*)
1½ ounces [50 g/5 cl] rose water
2 handfuls of untreated dried rose petals

Rinse the cherries in cold water and dry them in a towel. Stem and pit them. Combine them in a bowl with the sugar and lemon juice and let them macerate for an hour. Pour them into a preserving pan and bring to a simmer. Pour into a ceramic bowl. Cover with a sheet of parchment paper and refrigerate overnight.

Next day, put this preparation into a sieve. Pour the collected juice into a preserving pan. Add the apple jelly, bring to a boil, and boil 5 minutes. Skim carefully. Add the cherries. Return to a boil and cook on high heat about 5 minutes more, stirring gently. Skim again if necessary. Check the set. Add the dried rose petals and rose water. Return to a boil. Put the jam into jars immediately and seal.

* The Morello is a sour, dark cherry. In the United States, the Balaton cherry is a Morello varietal available in Michigan, a major cherry-producing state. Tart "pie" cherries may also be used. See Sources, page xi.

Morello Cherry and Black Cherry with Kirsch*

1⅓ pounds [625 g] Morello cherries, *or* 1 pound 2 ounces [500 g] net

1⅓ pounds [625 g] black cherries, *or* 1 pound 2 ounces net [500 g] net

3¾ cups [800 g] granulated sugar

Juice of 1 small lemon

7 ounces [200 g] Green Apple Jelly (*page 120*)

1 ounce [30 g/3 cl] kirsch

Rinse the Morello cherries and the black cherries in cold water and dry them in a towel. Stem and pit them. Combine them in a ceramic bowl with the sugar and lemon juice. After an hour of maceration, pour into a preserving pan and bring to a simmer. Pour into a ceramic bowl. Cover the fruit with a sheet of parchment paper and refrigerate overnight.

Next day, put the preparation into a sieve. Pour the collected juice into a preserving pan. Add the apple jelly, bring to a boil, and boil for 5 minutes. Skim carefully. Add the Morello and black cherries. Return to a boil and continue cooking on high heat for about 5 minutes, stirring gently. Skim if needed. Check the set. Add the kirsch. Put the jam into jars immediately and seal.

* The Morello is a sour, dark cherry. In the United States, the Balaton cherry is a Morello varietal available in Michigan, a major cherry-producing state. Tart "pie" cherries may also be used. See Sources, page xi.

Gariguette Strawberry*

2½ pounds [1.1 kg] Gariguette strawberries, or 2¼ pounds [1 kg] net
4 cups [850 g] granulated sugar
Juice of 1 small lemon

Quickly rinse the strawberries in cold water. Dry them in a towel and hull them. Let the strawberries macerate with the lemon juice and sugar in a ceramic bowl refrigerated overnight, covered with a sheet of parchment paper.

Next day, bring this preparation to a simmer in a preserving pan. Pour it into a ceramic bowl. Cover with a sheet of parchment paper and refrigerate overnight.

On the third day, pour this preparation into a sieve. Bring the collected syrup to a boil in a preserving pan, skim, and continue cooking on high heat. The syrup will be sufficiently concentrated at 221°F [105°C] on a candy thermometer. Add the partly cooked strawberries. Return to a boil on high heat. Skim and return to a boil for 5 minutes, stirring gently. Check the set. The strawberries will be translucent, like preserves. Put the jam into jars immediately and seal.

~:~

Gariguette strawberries are from Provence. They are the earliest to appear, in April. They are bright red and are considered the most flavorful and fragrant of all French strawberries—"incomparable."

---

* Where Gariguettes are not available, one may substitute any deeply fragrant and richly colored strawberry.

Wild Mara Strawberry and Wild Strawberry[*]

2½ pounds [1.1 kg] wild Mara strawberries, *or* 2¼ pounds [1 kg] net
9 ounces (*about 2½ cups*) [250 g] wild strawberries
4⅔ cups [1 kg] granulated sugar
Juice of 1 lemon

Quickly rinse the Mara strawberries under cold water. Dry them in a towel and hull them.

Let the Mara strawberries macerate with the lemon juice and the sugar in a ceramic bowl covered with a sheet of parchment paper in the refrigerator overnight.

Next day, bring this preparation to a simmer in a preserving pan with the washed and hulled wild strawberries. Then pour it into a ceramic bowl. Cover with a sheet of parchment paper and refrigerate overnight.

The third day, pour the preparation into a sieve. Bring the collected syrup to a boil in a preserving pan, skim, and continue cooking on high heat. The syrup will be sufficiently concentrated at 221°F [105°C] on a candy thermometer. Add the combined strawberry mixture. Bring to a boil again on high heat. Skim and return to a boil for about 5 minutes, stirring gently. Check the set. The strawberries will now be translucent, like preserves. Put the jam into jars immediately and seal.

~:~

Instead of making jam with wild woods strawberries alone, which are always a little bitter after they are cooked because they have so many seeds, I prefer to mix them with wild Mara strawberries. The Mara have the same delicate fragrance as wild woods strawberries.

---

* *Where Mara strawberries are not available, use local, wild strawberries combined with ripe, locally grown, domestic strawberries.*

Strawberry with Black Pepper and Fresh Mint

2½ pounds [1.1 kg] strawberries, *or* 2¼ pounds [1 kg] net
3¾ cups [800 g] granulated sugar
Juice of 1 small lemon
5 fresh mint leaves
5 black peppercorns, freshly ground

Quickly rinse the strawberries under cold water. Dry them in a towel and hull them.

Let the strawberries macerate with the lemon juice and the sugar in a ceramic bowl covered with a sheet of parchment paper overnight in the refrigerator.

Next day, bring the preparation to a simmer in a preserving pan. Pour it back into a ceramic bowl. Cover with a sheet of parchment paper and refrigerate overnight.

The third day, pour the preparation into a sieve. Bring the collected syrup to a boil in a preserving pan, skim, and continue cooking on high heat. The syrup will be sufficiently concentrated at 221°F [105°C] on a candy thermometer. Add the half-cooked strawberries from the sieve, fresh mint, and pepper. Return to a boil on high heat. Skim and bring back to a boil for about 5 minutes, stirring gently. Check the set. The strawberries will now be translucent, like preserves. Put the jam in jars immediately and seal.

Strawberry with Raspberry Juice and Balsamic Vinegar

1¾ pounds [800 g] wild Mara strawberries, *or* 1½ pounds [700 g] net*

1¼ pounds [500 g] raspberries

4 ¼ cups [900 g] granulated sugar

Juice of 1 small lemon

3½ ounces [100 g/10 cl] water

1⅔ tablespoons [25 g/2.5 cl] balsamic vinegar

5 peppercorns, freshly ground

Select small strawberries. Rinse them in cold water, dry them in a towel, stem them, and halve them. In a bowl, combine the strawberries, sugar, and lemon juice. Cover with a sheet of parchment paper and let them macerate refrigerated overnight.

Next day, turn the raspberries into a saucepan with the water, bring to a boil, and boil for a few minutes. Put this mixture through a chinois, pressing the fruit lightly with the back of a skimmer. Set the collected raspberry juice aside. Pour the macerated strawberries into a sieve. Bring the strawberry syrup to a boil in a preserving pan with the raspberry juice. Skim and continue cooking over high heat. The syrup will be sufficiently concentrated at 221°F [105°C] on a candy thermometer. Add the macerated fruit, pepper, and balsamic vinegar and bring to a boil once more; skim, return to a boil, and boil for about 5 minutes, stirring gently. Check the set. The strawberries will be translucent like preserves. Put the jam into jars immediately and seal.

* Where Mara strawberries are not available, use local, wild strawberries combined with ripe, locally grown, domestic strawberries.

Strawberry with Passion Fruit

2¼ pounds [1 kg] small wild Mara *or* Elsanta* strawberries,
   or 2 pounds [900 g] net
10 passion fruit
4¼ cups [900 g] granulated sugar
Juice of 1 small lemon
7 ounces [200 g] Green Apple Jelly (*page 120*)

Choose small strawberries. Rinse the strawberries in cold water, dry them carefully in a towel, and halve them. Combine the strawberries, sugar, and lemon juice in a bowl. Cover the mixture with a sheet of parchment paper and let themmacerate refrigerated overnight.

Next day, cut the passion fruit in two. Using a small spoon, collect the juice and seeds.

Pour the macerated fruit into a sieve. Bring the collected juices to a boil in a preserving pan, skim, and continue cooking on high heat. The syrup will be sufficiently concentrated when it reaches 230°F [110°C] on a candy thermometer. Add the strawberries, the juice and seeds of the passion fruit, and the apple jelly to the syrup and bring to a boil again. Skim and continue cooking on high heat for about 5 minutes, stirring gently. Skim again if necessary. Check the set. The strawberries will be translucent, like preserves. Put the jam into jars immediately and cover.

---

* Elsanta is a late summer strawberry. Where Mara strawberries are not available, use local, wild strawberries combined with ripe, locally grown, domestic strawberries.

Strawberry with Pinot Noir and Spices

1¾ pound [800 g] small strawberries, *or* 1½ pound [700 g] net

1¼ cup [300 g/30 cl] Pinot Noir

3¾ cups [800 g] granulated sugar

1 stick cinnamon

2 star anise

⅛ teaspoon [pinch] ground nutmeg

3 cloves

7 ounces [200 g] Green Apple Jelly (*page 120*)

Choose small berries. Rinse them in cold water. Combine the strawberries, sugar, Pinot Noir, and spices in a bowl. Cover with a sheet of parchment paper and let them macerate refrigerated overnight.

Next day, bring this mixture to a boil in a preserving pan, and then turn it into a bowl. Cover with a sheet of parchment paper and refrigerate overnight.

On the third day, pour the fruit mixture into a sieve. Bring the collected syrup to a boil in a preserving pan. Skim and continue cooking on high heat. The syrup will be sufficiently reduced at 221°F [105°C] on a candy thermometer. Add the half-cooked strawberries and the apple jelly. Bring to a boil on high heat once more, skim, return to a boil and boil for about 5 minutes, stirring gently. Check the set. The strawberries will be translucent, like preserves. Put the jam into jars immediately and seal.

Strawberry and Red Currant Jelly with Whole Strawberries and Pepper

2½ pounds [1.1 kg] strawberries, *or* 2¼ pounds [1 kg] net

4¼ cups [900 g] granulated sugar *plus* 2 cups [400 g]

Juice of 2 small lemons

2 pounds [900 g] red currants, *or* 1¾ pounds [750 g] berries, net,
   or 2 cups, 1 ounce [500 g/50 cl] juice

3½ ounces [100 g/10 cl] water

5 peppercorns, freshly ground

Quickly rinse the strawberries under cold water. Dry them in a towel and hull them. Let them macerate overnight with the juice from one lemon and 4¼ cups [900 g] sugar in a ceramic bowl covered with a sheet of parchment paper.

Next day, bring the strawberry preparation to a simmer in a preserving pan. Pour it into a ceramic bowl. Cover it with a sheet of parchment paper and refrigerate overnight.

On the third day, rinse the red currants in cold water, drain, and remove them from the stems. In a preserving pan, bring them to a boil with the water. Cover the pan and let them soften over a low heat for 5 minutes.

Collect the juice by pouring the currant preparation into a fine chinois sieve, and then filter it through cheesecloth. Pour the strawberry mixture into a sieve. Bring the accumulated syrup to a boil with the red currant juice, the juice of the second lemon, and 2 cups [400 g] sugar. Skim and continue cooking on high heat. The syrup will be sufficiently concentrated at 221°F [105°C] on a candy thermometer. Add the half-cooked strawberries and pepper. Return to a boil without stirring. Skim again if necessary. Remove the strawberries with a skimmer and divide them among the jars. Return to a boil for about 5 minutes, stirring gently. Check the set. Fill the jars with syrup and seal.

Strawberry with Elderberry Blossoms

2½ pounds [1.1 kg] small wild Mara strawberries, *or* 2¼ pounds [1 kg] net*
3¾ cups [800 g] granulated sugar
Juice of 1 small lemon
5 bunches fresh elderberry blossoms

Choose small strawberries. Rinse them in cold water, dry them carefully in a towel, and stem them. In a bowl, combine the strawberries, sugar, and lemon juice. Cover with a sheet of parchment paper and let them macerate refrigerated overnight.

Next day, bring the fruit mixture to a simmer in a preserving pan. Turn into a bowl. Cover with a sheet of parchment paper and refrigerate overnight.

On the third day, pick the elderberry blossoms and rinse them quickly in cold water. Dry them in a kitchen towel and remove the crown of petals and pistils from the stems. Put the strawberry mixture into a sieve. Bring the collected juice to a boil in a preserving pan, skim, and continue cooking over high heat. The syrup will be sufficiently concentrated at 221°F [105°C] on a candy thermometer. Add the half-cooked strawberries. Return to a boil over high heat, skim, and boil again for about 5 minutes, stirring gently. Check the set. The strawberries will be translucent, like preserves.

Add the elderberry flowers, and return to a boil. Put the jam into jars immediately and seal.

∽∶∾

I suggest you gather the elderberry flowers on the day that you make the jam because they wilt very quickly.

* Where Mara strawberries are not available, use local, wild strawberries combined with ripe, locally grown, domestic strawberries.

Spiced Green Walnut

---

5 pounds [2.2 kg] green walnuts, *or* about 2¼ pounds [1 kg] net

3¾ cups [800 g] granulated sugar

Juice of 1 small lemon

2 cinnamon sticks

½ teaspoon ground cardamom

7 ounces [200 g] **Green Apple Jelly** (*page 120*)

Collect the walnuts around mid-June; at that point they'll still be very soft and their brown shell won't yet be formed.

Peel the nuts, removing all the green skin. Heat a pan of water. Put in the nuts, bring to boiling, and boil a few minutes. Then rinse them in cold water and let them soak for 48 hours in a bowl filled with cold water.

The third day, drain the nuts, dry them in a kitchen towel and slice them thin. In a preserving pan combine the nuts, sugar, lemon juice, and spices. Bring to a simmer, then turn into a bowl. Cover with a sheet of parchment paper and refrigerate overnight.

On the fourth day, pour the mixture into a preserving pan, bring to a simmer, and then turn back into a bowl. Cover with a sheet of parchment paper and refrigerate overnight.

The fifth day, pour the mixture into a preserving pan, add the apple jelly, and bring to a boil; skim and continue cooking on high heat for 5 to 10 minutes, stirring gently. Check the set, remove the cinnamon sticks, and return to a boil. Put the jam into jars immediately and seal.

Apple Jelly with Fresh Mint

3⅓ pounds [1.5 kg] Granny Smith apples
6⅓ cups [1.5 kg/150 cl] water
4⅔ cups [1 kg] granulated sugar
Juice of 1 small lemon
1 small bunch fresh mint

Rinse the apples in cold water. Remove the stems and cut the fruit into quarters without peeling. Put the fruit into a preserving pan and cover it with the indicated water. Bring the mixture to a boil and let it simmer for 30 minutes on low heat. The apples will be soft.

Rinse the mint in cold water and set aside 20 leaves, wrapped in a damp cloth. Add the mint sprigs to the cooked apples and let the mint infuse for about 15 minutes. Then collect the juice by pouring the mixture into a fine chinois sieve and pressing the fruit lightly with the back of a skimmer. Filter it a second time, through cheesecloth, which you have wet and wrung out. Let the juice run freely. It's best to let the juice rest overnight in the refrigerator.

Next day, measure 4¼ cups [1 kg/1 l] of the juice, leaving in the bottom of the bowl the sediment that formed during the night. This will make for clearer jelly. Pour the juice into a preserving pan with the sugar and lemon juice and bring it to a simmer. Skim and continue cooking on high heat for 5 to 10 minutes, stirring gently. Check the set. Put a few of the reserved mint leaves in each jar. Put the jelly into the jars immediately and seal.

Depending on how you close the jars (see previous recipe), the mint leaves will come to the top or will stay in the bottom. When the jelly is lukewarm and almost set, shake each jar gently to distribute the leaves more harmoniously.

The indispensible
ingredient: lemon.

Strawberry and Red Currant Jelly with Whole Strawberries and Pepper (pages 30–31)

Rhubarb, Orange, and
Apple (page 40)

Rhubarb and Whole
Strawberries (page 42)

Apple Jelly with Rose Petals (pages 38–39), and Strawberry with Passion Fruit (page 28)

Morello Cherry with
Rose Petals (page 22)

Rhubarb, Apple, and
Passion Fruit (page 43)

Strawberry with
Pinot Noir and Spices
(page 29)

Rhubarb

2¾ pounds [1.2 kg] rhubarb, *or* 2¼ pounds [1 kg] net
3¾ cups [800 g] granulated sugar
Juice of 1 lemon

Rinse the rhubarb in cold water, cut the stems in two, lengthwise, and then in small dice. Macerate the rhubarb, sugar, and lemon juice overnight in a ceramic bowl covered with a piece of parchment paper.

Next day, pour this preparation into a sieve. Bring the collected juice to a boil in a preserving pan. Skim and continue cooking on high heat. The syrup will be sufficiently concentrated at 221°F [105°C] on a candy thermometer. Add the diced rhubarb. Return to a boil, mixing gently. Skim. Continue cooking on high heat for about 5 minutes, continuing to stir. Put the jam into jars immediately and seal.

~:~

I prefer rhubarb with slender, green stalks. It is less watery and slightly more acidic. I never peel it, so that the pieces will stay whole in cooking.

Apple Jelly with Acacia Flowers

3⅓ pounds [1.5 kg] Granny Smith apples
6⅓ cups [1.5 kg/150 cl] water
Juice of 1 small lemon
2½ cups [500 g] granulated sugar *plus* 2½ cups [500 g]
30 bunches acacia flowers

Rinse the apples in cold water. Stem them and cut the fruit into quarters without peeling them. Put the fruit into a preserving pan and cover them with the 6⅓ cups [1.5 kg/150 cl] water.

After bringing the apples to a boil, let them simmer for half an hour over low heat. The apples will be soft. Collect the juice by pouring this preparation into a fine chinois sieve, pressing lightly on the fruit with the back of a skimmer. Now filter again through a piece of cheesecloth that you have previously wet and wrung out. Let the juice run freely.

It's best to let the juice remain overnight refrigerated.

Next day, measure 4¼ cups [1 kg/1 l] of the juice collected, leaving in the bottom of the bowl the sediment that formed during the night, to have clearer jelly. Pour the juice into a preserving pan with 2½ cups [500 g] sugar. Prepare the acacia flowers, keeping only the pistil and the petals. Put them into the preserving pan. Bring to a simmer. Pour this preparation into a ceramic bowl. Cover with a sheet of parchment paper and refrigerate for 3 days.

Take the trouble to dry a few pretty bunches of acacia flowers over the 3 days.

The fourth day, pour the macerated, cooked mixture into a fine chinois sieve, letting the juice run freely. Pour the juice into a preserving pan. Add the lemon juice and 2½ cups [500 g] sugar. Bring to a boil, stirring gently. Skim. Continue cooking on high heat for 5 to 10 minutes. Check the set. Put the jelly into jars immediately, slipping one bunch of dried acacia flowers into each jar. Seal.

~:~

For beautiful clear jelly, the apple juice must be perfectly decanted, which means that the juice is separated from the solids in it, whether by filtering or by leaving sediment in the bottom of the container. You might also opt to preserve just the acacia petals and pistils in your jelly. Then you can use the dried flowers to decorate the outside of your jars.

~:~

The acacia flower has a very special perfume that reminds me of the first beautiful days of the year. Be careful to pick flowers that have just barely opened. The ones that are more open have already released the best of their fragrance.

Apple Jelly with Rose Petals

3⅓ pounds [1.5 kg] **green apples**

6⅓ cups [1.5 kg/150 cl] **water**

Juice of 1 small lemon

2½ cups [500 g] **granulated sugar** *plus* 2½ cups [500 g]

1 small basket untreated rose petals

3½ ounces [100 g/10cl] **rose water**

Rinse the apples in cold water. Stem them and cut the fruit in quarters without peeling. Put the fruit into a preserving pan and cover it with the water.

When it comes to a boil, let it simmer for half an hour on low heat. The apples will be soft. Collect the juice by pouring this preparation into a fine chinois sieve, pressing lightly on the fruit with the back of the skimmer. Now filter again with a piece of cheesecloth that you have wet and wrung out. Let the juice run freely.

It's best to let this juice remain overnight in the refrigerator.

Next day, measure 4¼ cups [1 kg/1 l] of the juice collected, leaving in the bowl the sediment that formed overnight, to have clearer jelly. Pour the juice into a preserving pan with 2½ cups [500 g] granulated sugar.

Set aside 1 handful of rose petals. Add the rest to the preserving pan. Bring to a simmer. Pour this preparation into a ceramic bowl. Cover with a piece of parchment paper and put aside for an hour.

Filter the macerated mixture through a piece of cheesecloth and let the juice run freely. Now pour the juice into a preserving pan. Add the lemon juice and 2½ cups [500 g] sugar. Bring to a boil, stirring gently. Skim. Continue cooking on high heat for 5 to 10 minutes. Check the set. Divide the reserved rose petals among the jars. Add the rose water to the jelly. Put the jelly into jars and seal.

Depending on the way you decide to close your jars—whether you turn them upside down or not—the petals will float to the surface or will stay at the bottom of the jar. When your jelly is nearly cool and almost set, gently shake each jar so the petals distribute themselves attractively.

Rhubarb, Orange, and Apple

½ pound [200 g] oranges

1 pound 9 ounces [700 g] rhubarb, *or* 1 pound 2 ounces [500 g] net

1¾ pounds [750 g] Ida Red apples*, *or* 1 pound 2 ounces [500 g] net

1 cup [200 g] granulated sugar *plus* 3¾ cups [800 g]

3½ ounces [100 g/10 cl] water

Juice of 1 small lemon

Wash the oranges in cold water and slice them into very thin rounds. In a preserving pan, poach the slices with 1 cup [200 g] sugar and the water. Continue cooking until the slices are translucent. Add the washed, unpeeled rhubarb, which has been cut into dice, and the apples, which have been peeled, cored, and cut into thin slices, the lemon juice, and sugar. Bring everything to a boil and cook 5 minutes, stirring gently.

Skim carefully, and return to a boil. Skim again, if needed. Check the set. Put the jam into jars immediately and seal.

* *Ida Red apples are large, bright red apples with firm, crisp, and slightly acidic white flesh.*

Rhubarb with Acacia Honey and Rosemary

2¾ pounds [1.2 kg] rhubarb, *or* 2¼ pounds [1 kg] net
2¾ cups [600 g] granulated sugar
7 ounces [200 g] acacia honey
Juice of 2 small lemons
10 sprigs rosemary

Rinse the rhubarb under cold water. Cut the stalks in two, lengthwise, and then in small dice. Let the rhubarb, the sugar, and the juice of 1 lemon macerate overnight in a ceramic bowl covered with a piece of parchment paper.

Next day, pour this preparation into a sieve. Pour the collected juice into a preserving pan and bring to a boil. Skim and continue cooking on high heat. The syrup will be sufficiently concentrated at 221°F [105°C] on a candy thermometer. Add the diced rhubarb. Bring to a boil and mix gently. Skim carefully. Add the juice of the second lemon and the rosemary sprigs. Continue cooking for about 5 minutes, continuing to stir. Check the set. Put the jam into jars and seal.

Rhubarb and Whole Strawberries

2¾ pounds [1.2 kg] rhubarb, *or* 2¼ pounds [1 kg] net
2½ pounds [1.1 kg] strawberries or 2¼ pounds [1 kg] net
3¾ cups [800 g] granulated sugar *plus* 3 ¾ cups [800 g]
Juice of 2 small lemons

Rinse the strawberries under cold water, drain, and hull them. Let them macerate with 3¾ cups [800 g] sugar and juice of 1 lemon overnight in a ceramic bowl covered with a piece of parchment paper.

Next day, pour this preparation into a sieve. Pour the juice into a preserving pan, bring it to a boil, and cook for 5 minutes. Pour the cooked juice onto the strawberries, cover with a piece of parchment paper and allow to macerate again overnight.

The third day, bring this mixture to a boil 5 times. Do this sequence again four times at 8-hour intervals. Then pour the strawberries into a sieve. Bring the collected syrup to a boil and cook for 5 minutes. Add the cooked strawberries. Return to a boil, stirring gently. Skim carefully.

Meanwhile, prepare a jam with the rhubarb, 3¾ cups [800 g] sugar, and juice of 1 lemon (*See page 39*). The rhubarb jam should be started at the same time as the strawberry preparation because the rhubarb needs to sit overnight and the two batches of jam need to be finished at the same time.

When the two batches of jam have been skimmed, mix them in one pan. Boil for 3 minutes. Skim again if needed. Check the set. Put the jam into jars and seal.

Rhubarb, Apple, and Passion Fruit

1⅓ pounds [600 g] rhubarb, *or* 1¼ pounds [500 g] net
1⅓ pounds [600 g] Granny Smith apples, *or* 1¼ pounds [500 g] net
5 passion fruit
2 cups [400 g] granulated sugar *plus* 2 cups [400 g]
Juice of 1 small lemon

Rinse the rhubarb in cold water. Cut the stems lengthwise into two pieces, and then into large dice. Peel the apples. Cut them in half, core them, and slice them into thin slices. Cut the passion fruit in half and collect the juice and the seeds. In a bowl macerate the diced rhubarb, 2 cups [400 g] sugar, and the lemon juice. In another bowl, macerate the apple slices, the juice and seeds of the passion fruit, and 2 cups [400 g] sugar. Cover each bowl with parchment paper and let them rest an hour.

Pour each preparation into a *separate* preserving pan and bring to a simmer. Turn once more into *separate* bowls and cover each mixture with a piece of parchment paper. Refrigerate overnight.

Next day, bring each mixture separately to a boil in a preserving pan; skim and continue cooking on high heat for about 5 minutes, stirring gently. Combine the two mixtures in one preserving pan. Skim again if need be. Return to a boil. Check the set and then put the jam into jars and seal.

Rhubarb, Apples, and Gewürztraminer

---

1 pound 2 ounces [500 g] rhubarb, *or* 1 pound [400 g] net

1 pound 2 ounces [500 g] Granny Smith apples, *or* 1 pound [400 g] net

3¾ cups [800 g] granulated sugar

7 ounces [200 g/20 cl] Gewürztraminer

Juice of 1 small lemon

Rinse the rhubarb in cold water, cut the stems in two lengthwise, and cut them into small dice. Peel the apples, cut them in half, core them, and cut them into small dice. In a bowl, combine the cut fruit, sugar, Gewürztraminer, and lemon juice. Cover with a sheet of parchment paper and let macerate overnight refrigerated.

Next day, turn this preparation into a sieve. In a preserving pan, bring the collected syrup to a boil, skim, and continue cooking on high heat. The syrup will be sufficiently concentrated at 221°F [105°C] on a candy thermometer. Add the macerated fruit and bring to a boil again on high heat. Skim, then return to a boil for 5 to 10 minutes, stirring gently. Check the set. Put the jam into jars and seal.

Rhubarb and Banana with Orange and Lemon Zest

1⅓ pounds [600 g] of rhubarb, *or* 1 pound 2 ounces [500 g] net

1 pound 11 ounces [750 g] bananas, *or* 1 pound 2 ounces [500 g] net

Juice and zest of 1 orange

Juice and zest of 1 lemon

4¼ cups [850 g] granulated sugar

Rinse the rhubarb in cold water. Cut the stems in two lengthwise, and then in large cubes. Peel the bananas and cut them into round slices a little less than ½-inch thick. With a brush, scrub the lemon and orange under cold water. Remove three strips of lemon rind and three strips of orange rind with a zester and cut the zest into fine slivers. Squeeze the orange and the lemon to collect the juice.

In a bowl, combine the cut fruit, sugar, juices, and slivered citrus zest and let them macerate an hour. Turn the preparation into a preserving pan and bring to a simmer. Turn again into a bowl, cover with parchment paper, and refrigerate overnight.

The next day, pour this preparation into a sieve. In a preserving pan, bring the juice collected to a boil; skim and continue cooking. The syrup will be sufficiently concentrated at 221°F [105°C] on a candy thermometer. Add the fruit pieces and bring once more to a boil on high heat. Skim and return to a boil for about 5 minutes, stirring gently. Check the set. Place the jam into jars immediately and seal.

Rhubarb and Apple with Beer

1 pound 2 ounces [500 g] rhubarb, *or* 1 pound [400 g] net

1 pound 2 ounces [500 g] Granny Smith apples, *or* 1 pound [400 g] net

4¼ cups [900 g] granulated sugar

1¼ cups [300 g/30 cl] light-colored beer

Juice of 1 small lemon

Rinse the rhubarb in cold water, cut the stems in two lengthwise, and then into small cubes. Peel the apples, halve them, core them, and slice them thin. In a bowl, combine the cut fruit, sugar, lemon juice, and beer. Cover with a sheet of parchment paper and macerate overnight refrigerated.

Next day, turn this preparation into a sieve. In a preserving pan, bring the juice collected to a boil; skim and continue cooking on high heat. The syrup will be sufficiently concentrated at 221°F [105°C] on a candy thermometer. Add the pieces of macerated fruit and bring the mixture to a boil once more on high heat. Skim and return to a boil for 5 to 10 minutes, stirring gently. Check the set. Put the jam into jars immediately and seal.

Rhubarb Jelly with Grapefruit Sections

1⅓ pounds [600 g] rhubarb, *or* 1 pound 2 ounces [500 g] net

1 pound 2 ounces [500 g] apples

4¼ cups [1 kg/1 l] water

4⅔ cups [1 kg] granulated sugar

2 small grapefruits, *or* a scant ½ pound [200 g] grapefruit sections, all white removed

Juice of 1 small lemon

Rinse the rhubarb in cold water, cut the stems in two lengthwise, and then into large dice. Rinse the apples in cold water. Remove the stems and cut the fruit into 8 wedges without peeling.

Put the fruit into a preserving pan and cover it with the water indicated. Add the lemon juice. Bring to a boil, letting the mixture simmer for 30 minutes on low heat. The fruit will be soft. Collect the juice by pouring the mixture through a chinois sieve, pressing the fruit lightly with the back of a skimmer. Then filter it a second time, pouring it through a piece of cheesecloth, which you have wet and wrung out. Let the juice run freely. It's preferable to let it rest overnight in the refrigerator.

The next day, measure 3⅓ cups [800 g/80 cl] of juice, leaving in the bowl any sediment that has settled overnight. This will make for a clearer jelly. Next, peel the grapefruits, removing the white pith. Carefully remove the sections. Be sure to collect all the juice. Pour the sugar into the preserving pan with the grapefruit juice and 8½ ounces [250 g/25 cl] of the apple/rhubarb juice. Bring to a boil, skim, and continue cooking. The syrup will concentrate sufficiently at 230°F [110°C] on a candy thermometer. Add the remaining apple/rhubarb juice and grapefruit sections. Bring to a boil on high heat, then skim and return to a boil for about 10 minutes, stirring gently. Check the set. Put the jelly into jars immediately and seal.

Summer

Bergeron Apricot

2½ pounds [1.15 kg] Bergeron apricots, *or* 2¼ pounds [1 kg] net
3¾ cups [800 g] granulated sugar
7 ounces [200 g/20 cl] water
Juice of 2 small lemons

Rinse the apricots in cold water. Cut them in half to pit them. Mix the apricots, sugar, water, and lemon juice in a ceramic bowl. Cover with a piece of parchment paper. Allow to macerate refrigerated for 8 hours.

Pour the contents of the bowl into the preserving pan and bring to a simmer. Return to the ceramic bowl. Cover with a piece of parchment paper and refrigerate overnight.

The second day, pour this preparation into a sieve. Remove the skin from the apricots. Bring the collected juice to a boil in the preserving pan. Skim, and continue cooking on high heat. The syrup will be sufficiently concentrated at 221°F [105°C] on a candy thermometer. Add the apricot halves. Boil again, skimming carefully. Lift out the apricots with the skimmer and divide them among the jars.

Continue cooking the syrup on high heat for about 3 minutes. Check the set. Finish filling the jars with the syrup and seal.

~:~

To make this jam, you need apricots that are ripe but firm. Apricots that are too juicy turn into mush when they are cooked.

Bergeron Apricot with Almond

2½ pounds [1.15 kg] Bergeron apricots, *or* 2¼ pounds [1 kg] net
3¾ cups [800 g] granulated sugar
7 ounces [200 g/20 cl] water
Juice of 1 small lemon
3½ ounces (*a scant cup*) [100 g] slivered almonds
Some apricot "almonds"*

Rinse the apricots in cold water. Cut them in half to pit them. Mix the apricots, sugar, water, and the lemon juice in a ceramic bowl. Cover with a sheet of wax paper and macerate in the refigerator for 1 hour.

Pour the macerated fruit mixture into a preserving pan and bring to a simmer. Pour back into the bowl. Cover with a sheet of parchment paper and refrigerate overnight.

Next day, pour this preparation into a sieve. Remove the skin from the half-cooked apricots. Bring the accumulated syrup to a boil in a preserving pan. Skim and continue cooking on high heat. The syrup will be sufficiently concentrated at 221°F [105°C] on a candy thermometer. Add the apricot halves and the slivered almonds. Boil for about 5 minutes, stirring gently. Skim carefully. Check the set.

Put the jam into jars immediately. Put a few apricot "almonds" into each and seal.

*Apricot "almonds" are the husked and skinned apricot kernels. However, apricot pits may be considered poisonous, containing small amounts of cyanide, although accidental poisoning from food sources is unlikely. Since concentrated amounts can kill, use these apricot "almonds" at your own risk. The reason it adds the bitter almond taste is because that is the flavor of cyanide. The original French ingredient list is included for authenticity, but readers are encouraged to use real slivered almonds rather than the suggested apricot kernels.

~:~

Use a nutcracker to remove the "almonds" or kernels from the apricot pits. Then put them into a pot of boiling water and remove their skins. Bring them to a boil again before adding them to the jam.

~:~

The apricot pits are added in this recipe to make your jam pretty. You could also replace all the slivered almonds with apricot "almonds." This will give a slight taste of bitter almond to your jam.

Bergeron Apricot with Vanilla

2½ pounds [1.15 kg] Bergeron apricots, *or* 2¼ pounds [1 kg] net
3¾ cups [800 g] granulated sugar
7 ounces [200 g/20 cl] water
Juice of 1 small lemon
2 vanilla beans

Rinse the apricots in cold water. Cut them in half to pit them. Mix the apricots, sugar, water, vanilla beans split lengthwise, and the lemon juice in a ceramic bowl. Cover with a piece of parchment paper. Refrigerate and macerate for an hour.

Pour the contents of the bowl into a preserving pan and bring to a simmer. Pour back into the bowl. Cover with a sheet of parchment paper and refrigerate overnight.

Next day, pour this preparation into a sieve. Remove the skins from the half-cooked apricots. Bring the collected syrup to a boil in a preserving pan. Skim and continue cooking on high heat. The syrup will be sufficiently concentrated at 221°F [105°C] on a candy thermometer. Add the apricot halves. Bring to a boil again and cook 5 minutes, stirring gently. Skim carefully. Remove the vanilla beans. They can be used to decorate the outside of your jars. Check the set.

Put the jam into jars immediately and seal.

Apricot with Mountain Honey

2½ pounds [1.15 kg] Bergeron apricots, *or* 2¼ pounds [1 kg] net

3 cups [600 g] granulated sugar

7 ounces [200 g] mountain honey

7 ounces [200 g/20 cl] water

Juice of 2 small lemons

Rinse the apricots in cold water. Cut them in half to pit them. Mix the apricots, sugar, water, honey, and lemon juice in a ceramic bowl. Cover with a sheet of parchment paper. Refrigerate and macerate for an hour.

Pour the contents of the bowl into a preserving pan and bring to a simmer. Pour back into the bowl. Cover with a sheet of parchment paper and refrigerate overnight.

Next day, pour this mixture into a sieve. Bring the accumulated syrup to a boil. Skim and continue cooking on high heat. The syrup will be sufficiently concentrated at 221°F [105°C] on a candy thermometer. Add the apricot halves. Boil for 5 minutes, stirring gently. Skim carefully. Check the set.

Put the jam into jars immediately and seal.

~:~

This jam will be a little more amber in color, because good mountain honey is dark.

Apricot with Diced Mango

2½ pounds [1.15 kg] Bergeron apricots, *or* 2¼ pounds [1 kg] net
3¾ cups [800 g] granulated sugar *plus* 3¾ cups [800 g]
3½ pounds [1.6 kg] mangoes, *or* 2¼ pounds [1 kg] net
7 ounces [100 g/10 cl] water
Juice of 2 small lemons

Rinse the apricots in cold water. Cut them in half to pit them. Mix the apricots, 3¾ cups [800 g] of the sugar, water, and lemon juice in a ceramic bowl. Cover with a sheet of parchment paper. Refrigerate and macerate for 8 hours.

Pour the contents of the bowl into a preserving pan and bring to a simmer. Pour back into the bowl. Cover with a sheet of parchment paper and refrigerate overnight.

The same day, peel the mangoes and remove their pits. Cut the flesh into small dice. Combine the mangoes and the remaining 3¾ cups [800 g] sugar in a preserving pan, and then bring to a simmer. Pour into a ceramic bowl. Cover with a sheet of parchment paper and refrigerate overnight.

Next day, pour the apricot mixture into a sieve. Remove the skins from the half-cooked apricots. Bring the collected syrup to a boil in a preserving pan. Skim and continue cooking on high heat. The syrup will be sufficiently reduced at 221°F [105°C] on a candy thermometer. Add the apricot halves. Return to a boil for about 5 minutes, stirring gently. Skim carefully.

Meanwhile, in another preserving pan, bring the mango preparation to a boil. Keep cooking on high heat for about 5 minutes, stirring and skimming carefully.

Now combine the two mixtures in one preserving pan. Bring to a boil. Skim if needed. Check the set. Put the jam into jars and seal.

Apricot and Raspberry with Citrus Zest

1⅓ pounds [600 g] ripe but still firm Bergeron apricots,
    or 1 pound 2 ounces [500 g] net
1 pound 2 ounces (*about 4½ to 5 cups*) [500 g] raspberries
2 cups [400 g] sugar *plus* 2 cups [400 g]
Juice of 1 small lemon
Finely grated zest of ¼ lemon
Finely grated zest of ¼ orange

Rinse the apricots in cold water, cut them in quarters, and remove the stones. In a bowl, combine the apricots, 2 cups of sugar, the lemon juice, and the citrus zest. In another bowl, combine the raspberries and 2 cups of sugar. Cover each bowl with a sheet of parchment paper and let the fruit macerate for 1 hour.

Pour each preparation into a separate preserving pan and bring to a simmer. Pour back into the bowls and cover each mixture with a sheet of parchment paper. Refrigerate overnight.

Next day, bring each mixture to a boil separately in preserving pans and continue cooking over high heat about 5 minutes, stirring gently. Combine the two mixtures in one preserving pan. Return to a boil, skimming again, if need be. Check the set and put the jam into jars and seal.

Apricot and Nectarine with Ginger

1⅓ pounds [600 g] ripe Bergeron apricots, *or* 1 pound 2 ounces [500 g] net

1½ pounds [650 g] nectarines, *or* 1 pound 2 ounces [500 g] net

3¾ cups [800 g] sugar

3½ ounces [100 g] finely chopped candied ginger

1 ounce [30 g] finely chopped fresh ginger

3 whole cloves

Rinse the apricots in cold water, cut them in quarters, and remove the pits. Blanch the nectarines for 1 minute in a pan of boiling water. Refresh them in a bath of ice water. Peel them and cut them in 10 sections. Remove the pits.

In a preserving pan, gently mix the apricot and nectarine sections, sugar, lemon juice, cloves, and fresh ginger. Bring to a simmer. Turn into a bowl, cover with a sheet of parchment paper, and refrigerate overnight.

Next day, pour this preparation into a preserving pan and add the preserved ginger. Bring to a boil, skim, and continue cooking on high heat for about 5 minutes, stirring gently. Check the set. Put the jam into jars and seal.

Nougabricot

2½ pounds [1.15 kg] ripe but still firm Bergeron apricots,
   or 2¼ pounds [1 kg] net
2¾ cups [650 g] granulated sugar
7 ounces [200 g] chestnut honey
Juice of 1 small lemon
Juice of 2 small oranges
3½ ounces (⅔ *cup*) [100 g] slivered almonds
3½ ounces (⅔ *cup*) [100 g] shelled, chopped pistachios
¼ teaspoon [2 pinches] finely grated orange zest

Rinse the apricots in cold water. Cut them in half to pit them. Mix the apricots, sugar, honey, orange juice, orange zest, and lemon juice in a ceramic bowl. Cover with a sheet of parchment paper. Refrigerate and let macerate for an hour.

Pour the contents of the bowl into a preserving pan and bring to a simmer. Pour back into the bowl. Cover again with a sheet of parchment paper and refrigerate overnight.

Next day, pour this preparation into a sieve. Remove the skin from the half-cooked apricots. Bring the collected syrup to a boil in a preserving pan. Skim and continue cooking on high heat. The syrup will be sufficiently concentrated at 221°F [105°C] on a candy thermometer. Add the apricot halves, the slivered almonds, and the chopped pistachios. Boil for 5 minutes, stirring gently. Skim carefully. Check the set. Put the jam into jars immediately and seal.

Two Kinds of Apricots
with Vanilla and Gewürztraminer

2½ pounds [1.15 kg] Bergeron apricots, *or* 2¼ pounds [1 kg] net

9 ounces [250 g] soft, dried apricots

3¾ cups [800 g] granulated sugar

Juice of 1 small lemon

Juice of 1 small orange

Finely grated zest of half an orange

2 vanilla beans

8½ ounces [250 g/25 cl] Gewürztraminer

Cut the dried apricots into little sticks a little less than $1/16$ inch [5 mm] wide, put them in a bowl, and cover them with the Gewürztraminer. Refrigerate overnight.

Rinse the apricots in cold water. Cut them in half to pit them. Mix the apricots, sugar, orange juice, orange zest, lemon juice, and vanilla beans split lengthwise in a ceramic bowl. Cover with a sheet of parchment paper. Refrigerate and let macerate for an hour.

Pour the contents of the bowl into a preserving pan and bring to a simmer. Pour back into the bowl. Cover with a sheet of parchment paper and refrigerate overnight.

The second day, pour the fresh apricot mixture into a sieve. Remove the skin from the half-cooked apricots. Bring the collected syrup to a boil in a preserving pan. Skim and continue cooking on high heat. The syrup will be sufficiently concentrated at 221°F [105°C] on a candy thermometer.

Add the dried apricots that have been macerated in the Gewürztraminer. Return to a boil and skim carefully. Add the apricot halves. Return to a boil for about 5 minutes, stirring gently. Skim again. Remove the vanilla beans, which you will use to decorate the outside of your jars. Check the set. Put the jam into jars and seal.

~:~

The Gewürztraminer selected for this recipe should have a heady nose with spicy tones: citrus fruits, candied dried apricot, gingerbread spices.

Spicy Apricot and Apple Jelly

2½ pounds [1.1 kg] apricots, *or* 2¼ pounds [1 kg] net

1 pound 2 ounces [500 g] homegrown green apples

4¼ cups [900 g] granulated sugar

4¼ cups [1 kg/1 l] water

Juice of 1 small lemon

Juice of 1 small orange

Finely grated zest of ½ orange

1 whole clove

½ stick cinnamon

⅛ teaspoon (*pinch*) gingerbread spice*

⅛ teaspoon (*pinch*) grated ginger

1 ounce [30 g/3 cl] Grand Marnier

Quickly rinse the apricots in cold water. Cut them in half to pit them.

Rinse the apples in cold water. Remove the stems and cut them into quarters without peeling or coring them. Put the apricots and apples into a preserving pan; cover them with the water and lemon juice. Bring to a boil.

Cover the pan and simmer on low heat for half an hour, stirring occasionally. Put this preparation into a chinois sieve and then filter it through a piece of cheesecloth, letting the juice run freely.

* Épices à pain d'épices, or gingerbread spice, is a blend of spices in which anise predominates, plus cinnamon and cloves. One might substitute apple pie spice, with a pinch of anise.

Pour the juice (4¾ cups [1.1 kg]) into a preserving pan with the orange juice, the orange zest, the sugar, and spices. Bring to a boil and boil 5 minutes. Skim carefully. Check the set. Remove the cinnamon stick and the clove and use small pieces of the cinnamon stick to decorate your jars. Add the Grand Marnier. Put the jelly into jars and seal.

~:~

You can make an excellent compote with the drained apples and apricots. Put them through a food mill with the coarse disk. Sweeten and spice to your taste.

Wild Blueberry*

2¼ pounds [1 kg] wild blueberries
3¾ cups [800 g] granulated sugar
Juice of 1 small lemon

Quickly rinse the blueberries in cold water. Drain them in a colander. In a ceramic bowl, mix them with the sugar and lemon juice. Let macerate for 10 minutes, then pour this mixture into a preserving pan and boil for 5 minutes, stirring gently. Pour back into a bowl. Cover with a sheet of parchment paper and refrigerate overnight.

Next day, bring the preparation to a boil again. Cook 5 minutes, stirring gently. Skim carefully. Check the set. Put the jam into jars immediately and seal.

~:~

You can serve blueberry jam as a garnish for apples or pears, baked in butter, with game. For this purpose, make it with 2¼ pounds [1 kg] blueberries and 2¾ cups [600 g] sugar, and add 3½ ounces [100 g] vinegar when it has finished cooking.

* The fruit specified in the French is airelle des bois—blueberry or huckleberry in North American English.

Blueberry Jelly*

Scant 4 pounds [1.75 kg] **blueberries**
2 cups 1 ounce [500 g/50 cl] **water**
4⅔ cups [1 kg] **granulated sugar**
Juice of 1 small lemon

Quickly rinse the blueberries in cold water. Drain them in a colander. Put the berries into a preserving pan and bring to a boil with the water. Cover the pan and let the berries soften on low heat for 10 minutes.

Collect the juice by putting this preparation into a chinois sieve, pressing the fruit with the back of the skimmer. Now filter again through cheesecloth that you have wet and wrung out. Pour the juice (4¾ cups [1.1 kg]) into a preserving pan with the lemon juice and sugar. Bring to a boil; cook 5 minutes. Skim carefully. Check the set. Put the jelly into jars immediately and seal.

* The fruit specified in the French is airelle des bois—blueberry or huckleberry in North American English.

Nectarines and Pears with Vanilla

1½ pounds [650 g] nectarines, *or* 1¼ pounds [500 g] net

1½ pounds [650 g] ripe but still firm William or Bartlett pears,
   or 1¼ pounds [500 g] net

3¾ cups [800 g] sugar

Juice of 1 small lemon

2 vanilla beans

Put the nectarines in a pan of boiling water for 1 minute. Refresh them in ice water. Peel them, cut them into 10 sections, and remove the pits. Peel the pears, stem them, core them, and slice them thin.

In a preserving pan, combine the nectarines, the pear slices, sugar, lemon juice, and vanilla beans split lengthwise. Bring the mixture to a simmer. Turn it into a bowl. Cover with a sheet of parchment paper and refrigerate overnight.

Next day, bring the mixture to a boil in a preserving pan. Skim and continue cooking on high heat for about 10 minutes, stirring gently. Remove the vanilla beans and return to a boil. Check the set. Put the jam into jars immediately and seal.

You can decorate each jar with a little piece of vanilla bean. This jam is delicious with whipped fromage blanc and a small *financier.**

*Small, buttery, almond cake.

Black Currant Jam

2¾ pounds [1.2 kg] black currant bunches, *or* 2¼ pounds [1 kg] net of berries
3¾ cups [800 g] granulated sugar
Juice of 1 small lemon

Rinse the black currants in cold water, drain them, and remove them from the stems. In a preserving pan, mix the black currants, sugar, and lemon juice. Bring to a simmer, then pour into a ceramic bowl. Cover the fruit with a sheet of parchment paper and refrigerate overnight.

Next day, put this preparation through a food mill (fine disk) to separate the skins and seeds.

In the preserving pan, bring to a boil, stirring gently. Continue cooking on high heat for about 5 minutes, stirring gently. Skim carefully. Return to a boil. Check the set. Put the jam into jars immediately and seal.

Black Currant Jelly

4¼ pounds [1.9 kg] black currant bunches, *or* 3½ pounds [1.6 kg] net of berries
1 cup [200 g/20 cl] water
4⅔ cups [1 kg] granulated sugar
Juice of 1 small lemon

Rinse the black currants in cold water; drain them and remove them from the stalks.

Put them in a preserving pan and bring to a boil with the water. Cover the pan and let the berries soften over low heat for 5 minutes.

Collect the juice by pouring this preparation into a chinois sieve and pressing the fruit with the back of a skimmer. Now filter the juice again through a piece of cheesecloth, which you have previously wet and wrung out.

Pour the juice (4¾ cups [1.1 kg]) into a preserving pan with the lemon juice and the sugar. Bring to a boil and continue cooking on high heat for about 5 minutes. Skim carefully. Check the set. Put the jelly into jars immediately and seal.

Crème de Cassis with Pinot Noir

2¾ pounds [1.2 kg] black currant bunches, *or* 2¼ pounds [1 kg] net of berries
8½ ounces [250 g/25 cl] Pinot Noir
4½ cups [950 g] granulated sugar
Juice of 1 small lemon

Rinse the black currants in cold water, drain, and stem them. In a preserving pan, mix the berries, sugar, and lemon juice. Bring to a simmer, and then pour into a ceramic bowl. Cover the fruit with a sheet of parchment paper and refrigerate overnight.

Next day, put the mixture through a food mill (fine disk) to separate the skins and seeds.

In the preserving pan, bring the mixture to a boil, stirring gently. Skim carefully. Add the Pinot Noir. Return to a boil and cook 5 minutes, stirring gently. Skim again if needed. Return to a boil. Check the set. Put the jam into jars immediately and seal.

Celery and Apples with Mountain Honey

2¼ pounds [1 kg] celery, or 1 pound 2 ounces [500 g] net
1½ pounds [650 g] Ida Red apples,* or 1 pound 2 ounces [500 g] net
3½ cups [750 g] granulated sugar
3½ ounces [100 g] mountain honey
Juice of 1 small lemon

Rinse the celery in cold water, peel it using a vegetable peeler, and cut it into fine julienne. Peel the apples, halve them, core them, and cut them in thin slices. In a bowl, combine the celery, sliced apples, sugar, honey, and lemon juice. Cover the bowl with a sheet of parchment paper and let the mixture macerate for an hour.

Pour the mixture into a preserving pan, bring it to a simmer, and pour it back into a bowl. Cover it with a sheet of parchment paper and refrigerate it overnight.

Next day, bring the preparation to a boil in the preserving pan, skim, and continue cooking on high heat for about 10 minutes, stirring gently. Check the set. Put the jam into jars and seal.

* Ida Red apples are large, bright red apples with firm, crisp, and slightly acidic white flesh.

Zucchini and Peppers with Spices

1¾ pound [750 g] zucchini, *or* 1⅓ pound [600 g] net

1 pound 2 ounces [500 g] peppers, *or* 1 pound [400 g] net

3¾ cups [800 g] granulated sugar

3½ ounces [100 g] floral honey

Juice of 1 small lemon

1 cup [150 g] pine nuts

½ teaspoon ground cardamom

Rinse the zucchini in cold water, peel them, and cut them in small dice. Rinse the peppers in cold water. Dry them in a towel and cut them in quarters. Set your oven to broil and broil the pepper quarters for a few minutes, cut face down. When they are wrinkled, you can easily remove the skin. Now dice them small. In a bowl, combine the diced squash and peppers, sugar, honey, lemon juice, and cardamom. Cover the bowl with a sheet of parchment paper and let the vegetables macerate 1 hour.

Pour the mixture into a preserving pan, bring it to a simmer, and pour it into a bowl. Cover with a sheet of parchment paper and refrigerate overnight.

Next day, bring the preparation to a boil in the preserving pan, skim, and continue cooking on high heat for about 15 minutes, stirring gently. Check the set. Add the pine nuts and return to a boil. Put the jam into jars immediately and seal.

Raspberry

2¼ pounds [1 kg] homegrown raspberries
3¾ cups [800 g] granulated sugar
Juice of 1 small lemon

Pick over the raspberries. Omit rinsing them so that they will keep their fragrance.

In a preserving pan, combine the raspberries, sugar, and lemon juice.

Bring to a boil, stirring gently. Continue cooking on high heat for 5 to 10 minutes, stirring and skimming carefully. Return to a boil. Check the set. Put the jam into jars immediately and seal.

Raspberry with Raspberry Eau-de-Vie

2¼ pounds [1 kg] raspberries

4¼ cups [900 g] granulated sugar

Juice of 1 small lemon

2 ounces [60 g] raspberry eau-de-vie

Pick over the raspberries. Omit rinsing them so that they will keep their fragrance. In a preserving pan, combine the raspberries, sugar, and lemon juice. Bring to a simmer. Pour into a ceramic bowl. Cover with a sheet of parchment paper and refrigerate overnight.

Next day, put the raspberries through a food mill (fine disk). Pour this into a preserving pan and bring to a boil and continue cooking on high heat for 5 to 10 minutes, stirring gently. Skim carefully. Check the set. Add the eau-de-vie. Put the jam into jars and seal.

Raspberry and White Peach

2¾ pounds [1.2 kg] homegrown raspberries, *or* 2¼ pounds [1 kg] net
4 cups [850 g] granulated sugar *plus* 3¾ cups [800 g]
Juice of 3 lemons
3 pounds [1.3 kg] homegrown white peaches, *or* 2¼ pounds [1 kg] net

Pick over the raspberries. Put them through a food mill (fine disk). In a preserving pan, mix the raspberry pulp, 4 cups [850 g] sugar, and the juice of 1 lemon. Bring to a simmer. Pour this mixture into a ceramic bowl. Cover with a sheet of parchment paper and refrigerate overnight.

Blanch the peaches by putting them into boiling water for 1 minute. Refresh them in ice water, peel them, pit them, and cut them into quarters.

In a preserving pan, combine the peaches, 3¾ cups [800 g] sugar and the juice of 2 lemons. Bring to a simmer. Pour into a ceramic bowl, cover the fruit with a sheet of parchment paper, and refrigerate overnight.

Next day, bring the mixtures to a boil separately, stirring gently. Continue cooking each one on high heat for about 10 minutes, stirring and skimming carefully. Check the set. Now combine the two preparations in one preserving pan. Return to a boil. Put the jam into jars immediately and seal.

Raspberry with Essence of Violet

2¾ pounds [1.2 kg] homegrown raspberries, or 2¼ pounds [1 kg] net
3¾ cups [800 g] granulated sugar
Juice of 1 lemon
3 drops essence of violet

Pick over the fruit. Put the raspberries through a food mill (fine disk). In a preserving pan, mix the pulp, sugar, and lemon juice. Bring to a boil, stirring gently. Keep cooking on low heat for 5 to 10 minutes, continuing to stir. Skim carefully. Return to a boil. Check the set. Add the essence of violet. Put the jam into jars immediately and seal.

~:~

Some varieties of raspberries, such as Meeker, have a violet fragrance when ripe . . . whence the idea for this combination.

Raspberry, Lemon, and Lemon Grass

2¾ pounds [1.2 kg] raspberries, *or* 2¼ pounds [1 kg] net

1 small lemon

Juice of 1 small lemon

25 fresh lemon grass leaves

3¾ cups [800 g] granulated sugar *plus* ½ cup [100 g]

3½ ounces [100 g] water

Pick over the raspberries. Omit rinsing them so as to keep their fragrance. Put the raspberries through a food mill (fine disk). Rinse and brush the lemon under cold water and slice it into very thin slices.

In a preserving pan, poach the lemon slices with ½ cup [100 g] sugar, the water, and lemon juice. Continue cooking until the slices are translucent. Add the raspberry pulp, 3¾ cups [800 g] sugar, and the lemon grass. Bring this preparation to a boil, stirring gently. Keep cooking on high heat for 5 to 10 minutes, stirring constantly. Skim carefully.

Remove the lemon grass leaves with a skimmer. Return to a boil. Check the set. Put the jam into jars and seal.

Raspberry with Chocolate

2¾ pounds [1.2 kg] raspberries, *or* 2¼ pounds [1 kg] net
3½ cups [750 g] granulated sugar
Juice of 1 lemon
9 ounces [250 g] extra bittersweet (68% cocoa) chocolate*

Pick over the raspberries. Omit rinsing them so as to keep their fragrance. Put the raspberries through a food mill (fine disk). In a preserving pan, mix the raspberry pulp with the sugar and lemon juice. Bring to a boil and cook 5 minutes, stirring gently and skimming carefully. Add the chocolate, grated. Mix and then pour into a ceramic bowl. Cover with a sheet of parchment paper and refrigerate overnight.

Next day, return the mixture to a boil. Continue cooking on high heat for about 5 minutes, stirring and skimming if needed. Return to a boil. Check the set. Put the jam into jars immediately and seal.

~:~

I use this technique of cooking the jam twice so that the chocolate and the fruit will combine nicely.

* An extra-bittersweet chocolate ranked high for quality and availability is Lindt's "Excellence." Excellence contains 70% cocoa, which makes it popular with professionals. Others are Callebaut, Tobler, Valrhona, and Ghirardelli. Bittersweet chocolate, called for in other jam recipes here, has 50% chocolate liquor and added cocoa butter content; extra-bittersweet begins at 65% chocolate liquor.

Raspberry, Morello Cherry, and Apple*

1⅓ pounds [600 g] Morello cherries, *or* 1 pound 2 ounces [500 g] net
1⅓ pounds [600 g] raspberries, *or* 1 pound 2 ounces [500 g] net
1⅓ pounds [600 g] Granny Smith apples, *or* 1 pound 2 ounces [500 g] net
5½ cups [1.2 kg] granulated sugar
Juice of 1 lemon
Zest of ½ lemon

Pick over the raspberries. Omit rinsing them so as to keep their fragrance. Put the raspberries through a food mill (fine disk). Wash the cherries. Dry them in a towel. Stem them and pit them. Peel the apples, remove the stems, core them, and cut them into thin slices.

In a preserving pan, mix the raspberry pulp, sliced apples, Morello cherries, sugar, lemon juice, and lemon zest. Bring to a simmer, then pour into a ceramic bowl. Cover the fruit with a sheet of parchment paper and refrigerate overnight.

Next day, bring to a simmer, continue cooking for 10 minutes on high heat, stirring gently. Skim carefully. Return to a boil. Check the set. Put the jam into jars immediately and seal.

* *The Morello is a sour, dark cherry. In the United States, the Balaton cherry is a Morello varietal available in Michigan, a major cherry-producing state. Tart "pie" cherries may also be used. See Sources, page xi.*

Raspberry with Star Anise

2¼ pounds [1 kg] raspberries
3¾ cups [800 g] sugar
Juice of 1 small lemon
4 star anise

Pick over the raspberries, but do not rinse them so that they keep their perfume. In a preserving pan, combine the sugar, lemon juice, and star anise. Bring to a simmer. Pour this mixture into a bowl, cover with a sheet of parchment paper, and refrigerate overnight.

Next day, bring this preparation to a boil in a preserving pan; skim and continue cooking on high heat for about 5 minutes, stirring gently. Remove the star anise and return to a boil. Check the set. Put the jam into jars immediately and seal.

Seedless Raspberry

2¾ pounds [1.2 kg] raspberries
4 cups [850 g] sugar
Juice of 1 small lemon

Pick over the raspberries, but do not rinse them, so that they keep their perfume. In a preserving pan, combine the raspberries, sugar, and lemon juice. Bring to a simmer. Pour this mixture into a bowl. Cover with a sheet of parchment paper and refrigerate overnight.

Next day, put the raspberries through a food mill (fine disk). Bring this preparation to a boil in a preserving pan, skim, and continue cooking on high heat for 5 to 10 minutes, stirring gently. Check the set. Put the jam into jars immediately and seal.

Raspberry and Litchi with Rose Water

1⅓ pound [600 g] litchis, *or* 1 pound [400 g] net

1⅓ pound [600 g] raspberries, *or* 1 pound [500 g] seeded

3¾ cups [800 g] sugar

Juice of 1 small lemon

7 ounces [200 g] **Green Apple Jelly** (*page 120*)

1½ ounces [50 g/5 cl] rose water

Peel the litchis and remove their stones. Pick over the raspberries, but do not rinse them, so that they keep their perfume. Put the raspberries through a food mill (fine disk). In a preserving pan combine the litchis, raspberry pulp, sugar, and lemon juice. Bring to a simmer. Pour this mixture into a bowl. Cover with parchment paper and refrigerate overnight.

Next day, bring this mixture to boil in a preserving pan and skim. Add the apple jelly. Return to a boil and continue cooking on high heat for about 5 minutes, stirring gently. Add the rose water and return to a boil. Check the set. Put the jam into jars immediately and seal.

Raspberry and Lemon with Elderberry Flowers*

2¼ pound (8 *to* 9 *cups*) [1 kg] raspberries
3¾ cups [800 g] sugar
1 lemon
5 fresh bunches of elderberry flowers

Sort the raspberries, but do not rinse them so that they keep their perfume. Rinse and scrub the lemon in cold water and cut it into very thin slices. Cut each round into quarters. In a preserving pan, combine the raspberries, sugar, and lemon pieces. Bring to a simmer, then turn this mixture into a bowl. Cover with a piece of parchment paper and refrigerate overnight.

Next day, gather the elderberry flowers and rinse them quickly in cold water. Remove the petals and pistils from the bunches. Put the raspberry/lemon preparation into a preserving pan. Bring to a boil, skim, add the elderberry flowers and pistils, and continue cooking over high heat for about 5 minutes, stirring gently. Check the set. Put the jam into jars immediately and seal.

*Creamy white flowers of the elder tree can be also be added to salads or batter-dipped and fried.

Raspberry Jelly

3⅓ pounds [1.5 kg] raspberries
4⅔ cups [1 kg] granulated sugar
Juice of 1 small lemon
7 ounces [200 g/20 cl] water

Sort the raspberries, but do not rinse them so that they keep their perfume. Pour the raspberries into a preserving pan and bring to a boil with the water. Cover the pan and let the fruit soften over low heat for 5 minutes. Collect the juice by pouring the preparation into a chinois sieve. To keep the jelly clear, do not press on the fruit. Filter the juice again by putting it through a piece of cheesecloth that you have wet and wrung out.

Pour the juice (4¾ cups [1.1 kg]) into a preserving pan with the lemon juice and the sugar. Boil for 10 minutes. Skim carefully. Return to a boil. Check the set. Put the jelly into jars immediately and seal.

Raspberry and Apple Jellies with Rose

For the raspberry jelly:

  1¾ pounds (*6 to 7 cups*) [750 g] raspberries
  2½ cups [500 g] granulated sugar
  Juice of ½ lemon
  3½ ounces [100 g/10 cl] water

For the apple jelly:

  1¾ pounds [750 g] homegrown green apples
  2½ cups [500 g] granulated sugar
  3 cups 2 ounces [750 g/75 cl] water
  Juice of ½ lemon
  3 tablespoons [50 g/5 cl] rose water
  A handful of dried, untreated rose petals

Prepare the raspberry jelly. Pour the raspberries into a preserving pan and bring them to a boil with the 3½ ounces [100 g/10 cl] water. Cover the pan and let the fruit soften on low heat for 5 minutes. Collect the juice by pouring the preparation into a fine chinois sieve. For clearer jelly, don't press on the fruit. Filter the juice again by pouring it through a piece of cheesecloth that you have soaked and wrung out. Pour the juice collected (2 cups 1 ounce [500 g/50 cl]) into a preserving pan with the juice of half a lemon and the sugar. Bring the mixture to a boil on high heat and cook for about 5 minutes. Skim and return to a boil. Check the set, and then fill each jar half full with the raspberry jelly.

Prepare the apple jelly. Rinse the apples in cold water. Remove the stems and cut the fruit into quarters without peeling it. Put the apples in a pan and cover them with the 3 cups 2 ounces [750 g/75 cl] water. When the preparation comes to a boil, let it simmer on low heat for 30 minutes. The apples will be soft. Collect the juice by pouring the mixture into a fine chinois sieve, pressing lightly on the fruit with the back of a skimmer. Now filter the juice again through a piece of cheesecloth that you have wet and wrung out. Pour the juice (2 cups 1 ounce [500 g/50 cl]) into a preserving pan with juice of half a lemon and the sugar. Bring to a boil and boil on high heat for about 5 minutes and then skim. Check the set. Add the rose water and return to a boil.

Sprinkle some dried rose petals on the partly jelled raspberry jelly and fill each jar the rest of the way up with the apple/rose water jelly. Seal immediately.

Red Currant

2¾ pounds [1.2 kg] red currants, *or* **2¼ pounds [1 kg] net**
3¾ cups [800 g] granulated sugar
Juice of 1 lemon

Rinse the red currants in cold water; drain them and stem them. In a preserving pan, mix the fruit, sugar, and lemon juice. Bring to a simmer, and then pour this mixture into a ceramic bowl. Cover with a sheet of parchment paper and refrigerate overnight.

Next day, put the mixture through a food mill (fine disk) to separate the seeds and skins.

In a preserving pan, bring the mixture to a boil, stirring gently. Continue cooking for 5 minutes, stirring constantly. Skim carefully. Return to a boil. Check the set. Put the jam into jars immediately and seal.

~:~

Take the time to stem the currants carefully, because the bits of stem will give a bitter taste to your juice.

Red Currant Jelly

4 pounds [1.8 kg] red currants, *or* 3⅓ pounds [1.5 kg] berries net
4⅔ cups [1 kg] granulated sugar
7 ounces [200 g/20 cl] water
Juice of 1 small lemon

Rinse the currants in cold water, stem them, and remove them from the stalks. Put them into a preserving pan and bring to a boil with the water. Cover the pan and let the berries soften over low heat for 5 minutes.

Collect the juice by pouring this preparation into a fine chinois sieve, pressing the fruit lightly with the back of the skimmer. Now filter the juice again by pouring it through a piece of cheesecloth that you have wet and wrung out. Pour the juice (4¾ cups [1.1 kg/110 cl]) into a preserving pan with the lemon juice and sugar. Boil for 5 minutes. Skim carefully. Check the set. Put the jelly into jars immediately and seal.

Red Currant Jelly with Lemon and Thyme Honey

4 pounds [1.8 kg] red currants, *or* 3⅓ pounds [1.5 kg] berries net

3¾ cups [800 g] granulated sugar *plus* ½ cup [100 g]

7 ounces [200 g/20 cl] water *plus* 3½ ounces [100 g/10 cl]

Juice of 1 small lemon

2 lemons

7 ounces [200 g] thyme honey

Sprigs of thyme in bloom

Rinse the currants in cold water, drain, and stem them. In a preserving pan, bring them to a boil with 7 ounces [200 g/20 cl] water. Cover the pan and let the berries soften on low heat for 5 minutes.

Collect the juice by pouring this preparation into a fine chinois sieve, pressing the fruit lightly with the back of the skimmer. Now filter the juice again by pouring it through a piece of cheesecloth that you have wet and wrung out.

Rinse and brush the lemons under cold water and cut them into thin round slices. In a preserving pan, poach the lemon slices with ½ cup [100 g] sugar and 3½ ounces [100 g/10 cl] water. Keep boiling until the slices are translucent. Add the currant juice, 3¾ cups [800 g] sugar, the thyme honey, and a few sprigs of thyme in flower. Bring this mixture to a boil. Continue cooking on high heat for about 10 minutes. Skim carefully.

Remove the thyme sprigs and lemon slices with the skimmer. Put them in the bottom of the jars. Return the jelly to a boil. Check the set. Finish filling the jars with the scented jelly and seal.

Gooseberry

2½ pounds [1.1 kg] gooseberries, *or* 2¼ pounds [1 kg] net
3¾ cups [800 g] granulated sugar
Juice of 2 small lemons

Wash the gooseberries in cold water. Drain them and dry them in a towel. Rub them in a dry towel to remove their fuzz. Remove the stems and any remaining blossoms.

In a preserving pan, mix the gooseberries, sugar, and lemon juice. Bring to a simmer. Pour into a ceramic bowl. Cover the fruit with a sheet of parchment paper and refrigerate overnight.

Next day, bring this preparation to a boil. Continue cooking on high heat for about 10 minutes, stirring gently. Skim carefully. Return to a boil. Check the set. Put the jam into jars immediately and seal.

Melon

4½ pounds [2 kg] melon, *or* 2¼ pounds [1 kg] net
3¾ cups [800 g] granulated sugar
Juice of 2 small lemons
2 vanilla beans
7 ounces [200 g] **Green Apple Jelly** (*page 120*)
1 lemon
1 orange
A pinch salt

Select perfectly ripe, very fragrant melons. Remove the rind and seeds. Cut the flesh into dice. In a ceramic bowl, combine the diced melon, sugar, lemon juice, and 1 vanilla bean split lengthwise. Allow to macerate for an hour.

Pour this mixture into a preserving pan and bring to a simmer. Pour back into the bowl, cover the fruit with a sheet of parchment paper, and refrigerate overnight.

Next day, cut wide strips of lemon and orange peel with a zester. Put them in boiling water with a pinch of salt for 5 minutes. Now rinse them in cold water and cut them into fine julienne.

Pour the melon preparation into a sieve and collect the juice.

In a preserving pan, bring the juice to a boil. Skim and continue cooking on high heat. The syrup will be sufficiently concentrated at 240°F [115°C] on a candy thermometer.

Now add the diced melon, the second split vanilla bean, the julienned peel, and the apple jelly. Bring to a boil and cook on high heat for about 10 minutes, stirring gently. Skim carefully. Remove the vanilla beans, which you'll use to decorate your jars. Return to a boil. Check the set. Put the jam in jars immediately and seal.

Melon with Almonds

4½ pounds [2 kg] melon, or 2¼ pounds [1 kg] net
4⅔ cups [1 kg] granulated sugar
13 ounces [350 g] almonds, freshly skinned, dried, and ground fine
Juice of 1 small lemon

Select perfectly ripe, very fragrant melons. Remove the rind and seeds. Cut the fruit into dice. In a ceramic bowl, mix the diced melon with the sugar and lemon juice and let macerate for an hour.

Pour into a preserving pan and bring to a simmer. Pour back into the bowl. Cover the fruit with a sheet of parchment paper and refrigerate overnight.

Blanch the almonds for 1 minute in boiling water. Lift them out with a skimmer and put them on a towel. Remove their skins and let them dry overnight.

Next day, put the melon through a food mill (fine disk). Grind the almonds fine. Pour the melon and the almonds into a preserving pan. Bring to a boil, stirring continuously. Skim carefully and continue cooking on high heat 10 to 15 minutes, still stirring. Skim again if needed. Check the set. Put the jam into jars immediately and seal.

Melon and Raspberry with Citrus Zest

---

3 pounds [1.4 kg] **melon,** *or* **1½ pounds** [700 g] **net**
1 pound [400 g] **raspberries,** *or* **¾ pound** [300 g] **seeded**
3¾ cups [800 g] **sugar**
Juice and finely grated zest of 1 lemon

Chose ripe fragrant melons. Cut them into eight wedges and remove the seeds. Remove the flesh and cut it into small cubes. In a bowl combine the melon, sugar, lemon juice, and zest. Cover the mixture with a sheet of parchment paper and let the fruit macerate for 1 hour.

Pour the mixture into a preserving pan and bring to a simmer. Put back into a bowl again, cover the fruit with a sheet of parchment paper, and refrigerate overnight.

Next day, put the raspberries through a food mill (fine disk) and set aside the pulp. Pour the melon preparation into a fine sieve. In a preserving pan bring the juice collected to a boil, skim, and continue cooking on high heat. The syrup will be sufficiently concentrated at 240°F [115°C] on a candy thermometer. Add the cubed melon and the raspberry pulp. Bring to a boil again on high heat, skim, and return to a boil for about 5 minutes, stirring gently. Check the set. Put the jam into jars immediately and seal.

Melon with Citrus and Candied Ginger

3½ pounds [1.6 kg] melon, *or* 1¾ pounds [800 g] net

3¾ cups [800 g] sugar

1 orange

1 lemon

3½ ounces [100 g] preserved ginger

Choose ripe and fragrant melons. Cut them into eight wedges and remove the seeds. Remove the flesh and slice the melon. Rinse and scrub the orange and the lemon in cold water, slice them into thin rounds, and cut each round into four. Remove the seeds. In a bowl combine the sliced melon and the citrus pieces and sugar. Cover the fruit with a sheet of parchment paper and let the fruit macerate for 1 hour.

Pour this preparation into a preserving pan and bring to a simmer. Return to a bowl, cover with a sheet of parchment paper, and refrigerate overnight.

Next day, pour the preparation into a fine sieve. In a preserving pan, bring the juice collected to a boil, skim, and continue cooking on high heat. The syrup will be sufficiently concentrated at 221°F [105°C] on a candy thermometer. Add the fruit and the preserved ginger, diced small. Bring to a boil once more on high heat, skim, and return to a boil for about 5 minutes, stirring gently. Check the set. Put the jam into jars immediately and seal.

*Green Melon with Lemon and Walnuts** *

3½ pounds [1.5 kg] melon, or 1¾ pounds [800 g] net

3 lemons

3¾ cups [800 g] sugar

7 ounces [200 g/20 cl] water

3½ ounces [100 g] floral honey

5 ounces [150 g] chopped walnuts

½ teaspoon, level, ground cinnamon

Cut the melon in eight wedges and remove the seeds. Remove the flesh and cut it into small cubes. Rinse and scrub the lemons in cold water. Cut them in thin round slices and cut each round into quarters. Remove the seeds. In a bowl, combine the diced melon, pieces of lemon, sugar, honey, cinnamon, and water. Cover with a sheet of parchment paper and let the mixture macerate overnight.

The next day, pour this preparation into a preserving pan, bring to a simmer, and turn into a bowl. Cover with a sheet of parchment paper and refrigerate overnight.

On the third day, pour this mixture into a fine sieve. In a preserving pan bring the syrup collected to a boil, skim, and continue cooking on high heat. The syrup will be sufficiently concentrated at 230°F [110°C] on a candy thermometer. Add the fruit, bring to a boil on high heat, skim, and return to a boil for about 5 minutes, stirring gently. Check the set. Add the chopped nuts. Return to a boil a final time. Put the jam into jars immediately and seal.

* The green melon, or melon vert, *describes several types of yellow skinned and fleshed melons. Any sweet, firm melon—Spanish melon, honeydew, canteloupe, cranshaw, Persian, or casaba—are good candidates for substitution.*

Mirabelle Plum

2½ pounds [1.2 kg] Nancy mirabelle plums, *or* 2¼ pounds [1 kg] net
3¾ cups [800 g] granulated sugar
Juice of 1 lemon

Rinse the mirabelles in cold water. Dry them in a towel and split them to remove the pits. In a ceramic bowl, combine them with the sugar and lemon juice. After 1 hour of maceration, pour contents into a preserving pan and bring to a simmer. Return to the bowl. Cover with a sheet of parchment paper and refrigerate overnight.

Next day, drain the fruit in a fine sieve. Bring the collected syrup to a boil and cook about 5 minutes: it should be sufficiently reduced at 221°F [105°C] on the thermometer. Add the plums, return to a boil, and keep cooking on high heat, stirring gently, for about 3 minutes. Skim carefully. Check the set. Put the jam into jars and seal.

⌒:⌒

I always use Nancy mirabelles. They are a pink-cheeked variety with an absolutely exquisite honey flavor. They have to be picked when they are ripe but still firm, or they'll lose texture in the cooking.

Mirabelle Plum with Orange and Cardamom

2½ pounds [1.2 kg] Nancy mirabelle plums, *or* 2¼ pounds [1 kg] net
1 cup [200 g] granulated sugar *plus* 3¾ cups [800 g]
2 oranges
3½ ounces [100 g/10 cl] water
Juice of 1 lemon
1½ teaspoons [3 g] ground cardamom

Rinse the oranges in cold water and slice them in very thin rounds. Rinse the mirabelles in cold water, dry them in a towel, and split them to remove the pits. In a preserving pan, poach the orange slices with 1 cup [200 g] sugar in the water. Keep cooking at a boil until the slices are translucent. Add the mirabelles, lemon juice, cardamom, and 3¾ cups [800 g] granulated sugar. Bring this preparation to a simmer and pour into a ceramic bowl. Cover with a sheet of parchment paper and refrigerate overnight.

Next day, bring to a boil again. Keep cooking on high heat for about 5 minutes, stirring gently and skimming carefully. Return to a boil. Check the set. Put the jam into jars immediately and seal.

Mirabelle Plum with Gewürztraminer and Vanilla

2½ pounds [1.2 kg] Nancy mirabelle plums, *or* 2¼ pounds [1 kg] net
4⅔ cups [1 kg] granulated sugar
1¼ cup [300 g/30 cl] Gewürztraminer
Juice of 1 lemon
3 vanilla beans

Rinse the mirabelles in cold water. Dry them in a towel and split them lengthwise to remove the pits. In a ceramic bowl, combine the prepared fruit with the sugar, lemon juice, and vanilla beans split lengthwise. Let macerate 1 hour, and then pour into a preserving pan. Bring to a simmer. Pour into a bowl. Cover with a sheet of parchment paper and refrigerate overnight.

Next day, bring this preparation to a boil and keep cooking on high heat about 5 minutes, stirring gently. Skim carefully, add the Gewürztraminer and return to a boil, cooking on high heat for about 5 minutes, stirring gently. Skim again and remove the vanilla beans. Check the set. Put the jam into jars immediately and seal.

The essential ingredient
with fruit: water.

Old Bachelor's Jam
(pages 112–13)

Raspberries, Yellow and White Peaches (pages 72 and 114)

Bergeron Apricot with
Vanilla (page 54)

*Apricot and Raspberry
with Citrus Zest
(page 57)*

*Melon and Raspberry
with Citrus Zest
(page 93)*

Raspberry and Litchi
with Rose Water
(page 81)

Alsatian Quetsch Plum
and Mirabelle Plum
with Cinnamon
(page 130)

Mirabelle Plum with Lemon and Tilleul (Linden) Honey*

2½ pounds [1.2 kg] Nancy mirabelle plums, *or* 2¼ pounds [1 kg] net

½ cup [100 g] granulated sugar *plus* 2⅓ cups [500 g]

3½ ounces [100 g/10 cl] water

2 lemons

Juice of 1 small lemon

8½ ounces [250 g] linden honey

Rinse and scrub the lemons in cold water and slice them into thin rounds. Rinse the mirabelle plums. Dry them in a towel and split them to remove the pits.

In a preserving pan, poach the lemon slices with ½ cup [100 g] sugar and the water. Cook at a boil until the slices are translucent. Add the plums, lemon juice, honey, and 2⅓ cups [500 g] sugar. Bring to a simmer. Pour into a bowl. Cover with a sheet of parchment paper and refrigerate overnight.

Next day, bring to a boil again and continue cooking on high heat for about 5 minutes, stirring gently. Skim carefully and return to a boil. Check the set. Put the jam into jars immediately and seal.

*Tilleul honey is from the blossoms of the lime tree (European); the American equivalent would be from the linden tree.

Mirabelle Plum and Chamomile

2¾ pounds [1.2 kg] Nancy mirabelle plums, *or* 2¼ pounds [1 kg] net

4⅔ cups [1 kg] granulated sugar

Juice of 1 small lemon

⅓ cup [30 g] chamomile flowers

8½ ounces [250 g/25 cl] water

Rinse the mirabelle plums in cold water, dry them in a towel, and split them to remove the pits. In a ceramic bowl, combine the prepared fruit with the sugar and lemon juice.

After 1 hour of maceration, pour contents into preserving pan and bring to a simmer. Pour back into the bowl. Cover with a sheet of parchment paper and refrigerate overnight.

Next day, bring this preparation to a boil and cook on high heat for 5 minutes, stirring gently. Skim carefully. Meanwhile, make an infusion with the water, heated, and the chamomile. Let it steep 5 minutes, then add the infusion to the jam. Return to a boil. Skim again if needed. Check the set. Put the jam into jars and seal.

Mirabelle Plum and Rhubarb

1⅓ pounds [600 g] mirabelle plums, *or* 1 pound 2 ounces [500 g] net
1⅓ pounds [600 g] rhubarb, *or* 1 pound 2 ounces [500 g] net
3¾ cups [800 g] sugar
Juice of 1 small lemon

Rinse the rhubarb in cold water, cut the stems in two lengthwise and then in small cubes. Rinse the mirabelle plums in cold water, dry them in a towel, and split them to remove the stones. In a bowl, combine the cut fruit, sugar, and lemon juice and let them macerate for 1 hour. Bring the mixture to a simmer in a preserving pan. Turn it into a bowl, cover with a sheet of parchment paper, and refrigerate overnight.

Next day, pour this mixture into a sieve. In a preserving pan, bring the accumulated syrup to a boil. Skim and continue cooking on high heat. The syrup should be sufficiently concentrated at 221°F [105°C] on a candy thermometer. Add the plums and the diced rhubarb and bring to a boil over high heat, boiling for about 5 minutes, stirring gently. Skim again if need be. Check the set. Put the jam into jars immediately and seal.

Wild Blackberry

2¼ pounds [1 kg] **wild blackberries**
3¾ cups [800 kg] **granulated sugar**
Juice of 1 small lemon

Pick over the blackberries. Rinse them quickly in cold water without soaking them. In a preserving pan, combine the blackberries, sugar, and lemon juice. Bring to a simmer. Pour into a ceramic bowl. Cover the fruit with a sheet of parchment paper and refrigerate overnight.

Next day, bring this preparation to a boil, stirring gently. Continue cooking on high heat for 5 to 10 minutes, stirring and skimming carefully. Return to a boil. Check the set. Put the jam into jars immediately and seal.

Wild Blackberry and Wild Raspberry

1 pound 2 ounces [500 kg] wild blackberries
1 pound 5 ounces [600 g] wild raspberries, *or* 1 pound 2 ounces [500 g] net
3¾ cups [800 g] granulated sugar
Juice of 1 small lemon

Rinse the berries quickly in cold water without soaking them. Drain them. Put the raspberries through a food mill (fine disk) to purée them.

Put the blackberries, raspberry puree, sugar, and lemon juice in a preserving pan. Bring to a boil, stirring gently. Continue cooking on high heat for 10 minutes, stirring and skimming carefully. Return to a boil. Check the set. Put the jam into jars immediately and seal.

A Trio of Wild Berries

---

1 pound 2 ounces [500 g] wild blackberries
1 pound 2 ounces [500 g] wild raspberries
1 pound 2 ounces [500 g] wild blueberries
3¾ cups [800 g] granulated sugar *plus* 2 cups [400 g]
Juice of 1 small lemon

Quickly rinse the blueberries in cold water without soaking them. Bring the blueberries and 2 cups [400 g] sugar to a simmer in a preserving pan. Pour this mixture into a ceramic bowl. Cover with a sheet of parchment paper and refrigerate overnight.

Quickly rinse the blackberries and the raspberries in the same way. In another preserving pan, bring them to a simmer with 3¾ cups [800 g] sugar. Pour this mixture into a ceramic bowl. Cover with a sheet of parchment paper and refrigerate overnight.

Next day, put the blackberries and raspberries through a food mill (fine disk) to separate the seeds. Pour the pulp into the preserving pan with the blueberries and the lemon juice. Bring to a boil, stirring gently. Continue cooking on high heat for about 5 minutes, stirring constantly and skimming carefully. Return to a boil. Check the set. Put the jam into jars immediately and seal.

Wild Blackberry and Vineyard Peach

2¼ pounds [1 kg] wild blackberries
3 pounds [1.3 kg] small vineyard peaches, *or* 2¼ pounds [1 kg] net
4 cups [850 g] granulated sugar plus 3¾ cups [800 g]
Juice of 2 small lemons

Pick over the blackberries. Rinse them quickly in cold water without soaking them. Put the blackberries, 4 cups [850 g] sugar, and lemon juice in a preserving pan. Bring to a simmer. Pour into a ceramic bowl, cover with a sheet of parchment paper and refrigerate overnight.

Put the peaches in boiling water for 1 minute. Refresh them in ice water, peel them, pit them, and cut them into quarters.

In a preserving pan, mix the peaches, 3¾ cups [800 g] granulated sugar, and the juice of 1 lemon. Bring to a simmer. Pour into a ceramic bowl. Cover with a sheet of parchment paper and refrigerate overnight.

Next day, put the blackberries through a food mill (fine disk) to remove the seeds. Now bring the peach mixture and the blackberry mixture to a boil in separate preserving pans, stirring gently. Continue cooking on high heat for about 5 minutes, stirring and skimming carefully. Check the set. Combine the two preparations in one pan. Return to a boil. Check the set. Put the jam into jars and seal.

Wild Blackberry Jelly

---

4 pounds [1.8 kg] wild blackberries
4⅔ cups [1 kg] granulated sugar
7 ounces [200 g/20 cl] water
Juice of 1 small lemon

Rinse the blackberries in cold water without soaking them. Pour them into a preserving pan and bring to a boil with the water. Cover the pan and let the fruit soften for 5 minutes. Collect the juice by pouring the preparation into a chinois sieve, pressing the fruit lightly with the back of the skimmer. Filter the juice again by putting it through a piece of cheesecloth that you have wet and wrung out.

Pour the juice (4¾ cups [1.1 kg]) in a preserving pan with the lemon juice and the sugar. Bring to a boil and cook for 5 minutes. Skim carefully. Return to a boil. Check the set. Put the jam into jars immediately and seal.

Wild Blueberry*

2¼ pounds [1 kg] wild blueberries
3¾ cups [800 g] granulated sugar
Juice of 1 small lemon

Rinse the blueberries in cold water without soaking them. Put them in a preserving pan with the sugar and lemon juice and bring to a simmer. Pour this mixture into a ceramic bowl. Cover with a sheet of parchment paper and refrigerate overnight.

Next day, bring the mixture to a boil, stirring gently. Continue cooking on high heat for 5 to 10 minutes, continuing to stir. Skim carefully. Return to a boil. Check the set. Put the jam into jars immediately and seal.

* The fruit specified in the French is myrtilles des bois—the bilberry or whinberry, known in North America as blueberry. This wild blueberry jam also differs slightly in technique from the recipe on page 64.

Wild Blueberry with Pinot Noir and Licorice*

2¼ pounds [1 kg] wild blueberries
8½ ounces [250 g/25 cl] Pinot Noir
4⅔ cups [1 kg] granulated sugar
Juice of 1 small lemon
2 sticks licorice root with many slashes made in them

Rinse the blueberries in cold water without soaking them. In a preserving pan, bring the blueberries to a simmer with the sugar, lemon juice, and licorice. Pour this mixture into a ceramic bowl. Cover with a sheet of parchment paper and refrigerate overnight.

Next day, bring the preparation to a boil, stirring gently. Continue cooking on high heat for about 10 minutes, continuing to stir. Skim carefully. Add the Pinot Noir. Return to a boil. Skim if needed. Remove the licorice. Check the set. Put the jam into jars and seal.

* "Licorice" candy is usually made with synthetic flavoring agents. To flavor this jam, professionals would use a piece of real licorice root, available at Chinese herbalists or health food stores, or confectioners' licorice that is prepared in small bars or powder.

Wild Blueberry and Lemon

2¼ pounds [1 kg] wild blueberries

4⅔ cups [1 kg] granulated sugar *plus* ½ cup [100 g]

3½ ounces [100 g/10 cl] water

7 ounces [200 g/20 cl] lemon juice

2 lemons

Rinse the 2 lemons in cold water and slice them into thin rounds. In a preserving pan poach the lemon slices with ½ cup [100 g] sugar and the water. Continue cooking until the slices are translucent.

Rinse the blueberries in cold water without soaking them. Add the blueberries, 4⅔ cups [1 kg] sugar, and the lemon juice to the pan and bring to a simmer. Pour into a ceramic bowl. Cover with a sheet of parchment paper and refrigerate overnight.

Next day, bring this preparation to a boil, stirring gently. Continue cooking on high heat for about 10 minutes, continuing to stir. Skim carefully. Return to a boil. Check the set. Put the jam into jars immediately and seal.

*Blueberry Jelly**

4 pounds [1.8 kg] blueberries
4⅔ cups [1 kg] granulated sugar
1 cup [250 g/25 cl] water
Juice of 1 small lemon

Rinse the blueberries in cold water without soaking them. Pour them into a preserving pan and bring to a boil with the water. Cover the pan and allow the fruit to soften on low heat for 5 minutes.

Collect the juice by pouring this preparation into a chinois sieve, pressing the fruit lightly with the back of a skimmer. Filter the juice again by pouring it through cheesecloth that you have wet and wrung out.

Pour the juice (4¾ cups [1.1 kg/110 cl]) into a preserving pan with the lemon juice and sugar. Bring to a boil and continue cooking on high heat for 5 to 10 minutes. Skim carefully. Return to a boil. Check the set. Put the jelly in jars immediately and seal.

* The fruit specified in the French is myrtilles des bois—the bilberry or whinberry, known in North America as blueberry. This wild blueberry jelly also differs slightly in technique from the Blueberry Jelly on page 65.

Watermelon, Apples, and Grapefruit

3 pounds [1.4 kg] watermelon, *or* 1½ pounds [700 g] net
¾ pound [300 g] Ida Red apples,* *or* ½ pound [200 g] net
1 pink grapefruit
4 cups [850 g] granulated sugar
Juice of 1 small lemon

Cut the watermelon in quarters, remove the skin and seeds, and cut the flesh into small cubes. Peel the apples, cut them in half, core them, and cut them into slices. Rinse the grapefruit and scrub it with a brush in cold water. Halve it, and then slice it thinly. Remove the seeds. In a bowl, combine the watermelon, sliced apples, grapefruit, sugar, and lemon juice. Cover the fruit with a sheet of parchment paper and let it macerate overnight.

The next day, turn this mixture into a preserving pan, bring to a simmer, and pour into a bowl. Cover with a sheet of parchment paper and refrigerate overnight.

On the third day, pour the mixture into a sieve. In a preserving pan bring the collected syrup to a boil; skim and continue cooking on high heat. The syrup will be sufficiently concentrated at 221°F [105°C] on a candy thermometer. Add the fruits, bring to a boil again on high heat, skim, and return to a boil for about 5 minutes, stirring gently. Check the set. Put the jam into jars immediately and seal.

* Ida Red apples are large, bright red apples with firm, crisp, and slightly acidic white flesh.

Old Bachelor's Jam with Wild Blueberries, Raspberries, and Kirsch

2¼ pounds [1 kg] wild blueberries
2¼ pounds [1 kg] raspberries
3¾ cups [800 g] granulated sugar *plus* 3¾ cups [800 g]
Juice of 1 small lemon
2 ounces [60 g/6 cl] kirsch

Quickly rinse the blueberries in cold water without soaking them. In a preserving pan, combine the blueberries, 3¾ cups [800 g] sugar and juice of half a lemon. Bring to a simmer. Pour this mixture into a ceramic bowl. Cover with a sheet of parchment paper and refrigerate overnight.

Quickly rinse the raspberries the same way. In another preserving pan, bring them to a simmer with 3¾ cups [800 g] sugar and the juice of half a lemon. Pour this mixture into a ceramic bowl. Cover with a sheet of parchment paper and refrigerate overnight.

Next day, bring the blueberries to a boil, stirring gently. Continue cooking on high heat for about 10 minutes, continuing to stir, and skimming if needed. Check the set. Put the jam into jars immediately, filling them just half. Let the jam jell.

For the final step, bring the raspberry mixture to a boil, stirring gently and skimming carefully. Continue cooking on high heat for about 5 minutes stirring and skimming carefully. Check the set. Off heat, add the kirsch, and finish filling the jars. Add one or two drops of kirsch to each jar and seal.

~:~

You can use wild blackberries instead of blueberries.

~:~

It used to be that every household would make Old Bachelor's Jam with a fruit and alcohol base. In Alsace, whenever people picked red and black fruit in their gardens or in the woods, they would add a few handfuls to a big crock, covering the fruit as they went along with sugar and kirsch. By fall, they could be enjoying this compote with crisp cookies, semolina pudding, or farmer's cheese.

Yellow and White Peach

1½ pounds [650 g] yellow peaches, *or* 1 pound 2 ounces [500 g] net
1½ pounds [650 g] white peaches, *or* 1 pound 2 ounces [500 g] net
3¾ cups [800 g] granulated sugar
Juice of 1 small lemon

Blanch the yellow and the white peaches for 1 minute in a pot of boiling water. Refresh them in ice water. Peel them and cut them into thick slices.

In a preserving pan, combine the peach slices, sugar, and lemon juice. Bring to a simmer, and then pour into a ceramic bowl. Cover the fruit with a sheet of parchment paper and refrigerate overnight.

Next day, pour this preparation into a sieve. In a preserving pan, bring the collected syrup to a boil and cook for 5 minutes: it should be sufficiently reduced at 221°F [105°C] on a candy thermometer. Add the peach slices and return to a boil, cooking on high heat for about 5 minutes, stirring gently. Skim again if necessary. Check the set. Put the jam in jars immediately and seal.

~:~

The peaches that you pick in your own garden are not as pretty to look at but are much more flavorful, so they will make wonderful jam. They are usually smaller and less gorged with juice, which makes them better for cooking. Also, garden peaches gel more quickly.

White Peach with Rose de Chine Tea

---

3 pounds [1.3 kg] white peaches, *or* 2¼ pounds [1 kg] net
3¾ cups [800 g] granulated sugar
Juice of 1 small lemon
3½ tablespoons [25 g] *rose de chine* (hibiscus) tea
7 ounces [200 g/20 cl] water
Handful of fresh, untreated rose petals

Blanch the white peaches for 1 minute in a pot of boiling water. Refresh them in ice water. Peel them and cut them into slices.

In a preserving pan, mix the peach slices, sugar, and lemon juice. Bring to a simmer, then pour into a ceramic bowl. Cover the fruit with a sheet of parchment paper and refrigerate overnight.

Next day, pour this preparation into a sieve. In a preserving pan, bring the collected syrup to a boil. Skim and cook on high heat. The syrup should be sufficiently concentrated at 221°F [105°C] on a candy thermometer.

Meanwhile, make an infusion with the water and the tea: let it steep for 3 minutes.

Add the peach slices and the tea to the cooking syrup. Return this to a boil and cook on high heat for about 5 minutes, stirring gently. Skim carefully. Add the rose petals. Return to a boil. Check the set. Put the jam in jars immediately and seal.

White Peaches with Saffron

A scant 3 pounds [1.3 kg] white peaches, *or* 2¼ pounds [1 kg] net
3¾ cups [800 g] granulated sugar
Juice of 1 small lemon
15 threads saffron

Blanch the white peaches for 1 minute in a pan of boiling water. Refresh them in ice water. Peel and halve them. Remove the pits and slice the peach halves. In a preserving pan, combine the peach slices, sugar, lemon juice, and saffron. Bring to a simmer, and then turn into a bowl. Cover the fruit with a sheet of parchment paper and refrigerate overnight.

Next day, pour this mixture through a sieve. Bring the collected syrup to a boil in a preserving pan, skim, and continue cooking on high heat. The syrup should be sufficiently concentrated at 221°F [105°C] on a candy thermometer. Add the sliced peaches and bring to a boil on high heat, boiling for about 5 minutes, stirring gently. Skim again if need be. Check the set. Put the jam into jars immediately and seal.

White Peach with Lemon Verbena

A scant 3 pounds [1.3 kg] white peaches, *or* 2¼ pounds [1 kg] net
3¾ cups [800 g] sugar
Juice of 1 lemon
Finely grated zest of half a lemon
10 sprigs of lemon verbena

Blanch the white peaches in a pan of boiling water for 1 minute. Refresh them in ice water. Peel and halve them. Remove the pits and cut the peach halves into slices. In a preserving pan combine the sliced peaches, sugar, lemon juice and zest, and 6 sprigs of lemon verbena. Bring the mixture to a simmer, and then turn it into a bowl. Cover the fruit with a piece of parchment paper and refrigerate it overnight.

Next day, put the preparation into a sieve. Bring the syrup collected to a boil in a preserving pan, skim, and continue cooking on high heat. The syrup will be sufficiently concentrated at 221°F [105°C] on a candy thermometer. Remove the sprigs of lemon verbena. Add the sliced peaches and bring the mixture to a boil over high heat, boiling for about 5 minutes and stirring gently. Add 20 lemon verbena leaves. Return to a boil. Check the set. Put the jam into jars immediately and seal.

Yellow Peach with Lavender Honey

---

3 pounds [1.3 kg] yellow peaches, or 2¼ pounds [1 kg] net
2⅓ cups [500 g] granulated sugar
1¼ cups [300 g] lavender honey
5 sprigs fresh, aromatic lavender
5 sprigs dried lavender
Juice of 1 small lemon

Blanch the yellow peaches 1 minute in a pan of boiling water. Refresh them in ice water. Peel them and cut them into dice.

In a preserving pan, combine the diced peaches, sugar, lavender honey, lemon juice, and the fresh lavender tied in a muslin bag. Bring to a simmer, and then pour the mixture into a ceramic bowl. Cover the fruit with a sheet of parchment paper and refrigerate overnight.

Next day, pour this preparation into a sieve. In a preserving pan, bring the collected syrup to a boil. Skim and continue cooking on high heat. The syrup should be sufficiently concentrated at 221°F [105°C] on a candy thermometer. Add the diced peaches. Return to a boil and cook on high heat for about 5 minutes, stirring gently. Skim carefully. Return to a boil. Check the set. Put the jam in jars immediately. Decorate the outside of each jar with a sprig of dried lavender and seal.

~:~

This jam will have a consistency a little like honey.

Yellow Peach and Orange

---

3 pounds [1.3 kg] yellow peaches, *or* 2¼ pounds [1 kg] net
3¾ cups [800 g] granulated sugar *plus* 1 cup [200 g]
1 orange
Juice of 1 small orange
Juice of 1 small lemon
3½ ounces [100 g/10 cl] water

Rinse and brush the orange under cold water and slice it into very thin rounds. In a preserving pan, poach the slices with the orange juice, 1 cup [200 g] sugar, and the water. Continue boiling until the slices are translucent.

Blanch the yellow peaches 1 minute in a pan of boiling water. Refresh them in ice water. Peel them and cut them into slices.

In a preserving pan, combine the peach slices, 3¾ cups [800 g] sugar, and lemon juice with the orange slices. Bring to a simmer, and then pour this mixture into a ceramic bowl. Cover the fruit with a sheet of parchment paper and refrigerate overnight.

Next day, pour this preparation into a sieve. In a preserving pan, bring the collected syrup to a boil. Skim and continue cooking on high heat. The syrup should be sufficiently concentrated at 221°F [105°C] on a candy thermometer. Add the peach slices and the orange slices. Return to a boil and continue cooking on high heat for about 5 minutes, stirring gently. Skim carefully. Return to a boil once more. Check the set. Put the jam in jars immediately and seal.

Green Apple Jelly

3⅓ pounds [1.5 kg] **green apples**
4⅔ cups [1 kg] **granulated sugar**
6⅓ cups [1.5 kg/150 cl] **water**
Juice of 1 small lemon

Rinse the apples in cold water. Remove the stem and cut the fruit into quarters without peeling them. Put them in a pan and cover them with the water. When the apple mixture comes to a boil, simmer for half an hour on low heat.

Collect the juice by pouring the preparation into a fine chinois sieve and pressing lightly on the fruit with the back of a skimmer. Now filter it a second time through cheesecloth, which you have wet and wrung out.

Pour 4¼ cups [1 kg/1 l] of the juice into a preserving pan with the lemon juice and the sugar. Bring to a boil, skim, and continue cooking on high heat for 5 to 10 minutes. Skim again if necessary. Return to a boil. Check the set. Pour the jelly into jars and seal.

~:~

This is the "pectin stock" jelly that you can add to jams such as pear or cherry that have very little natural pectin: it will facilitate the jell. Choose very green apples, preferably at the beginning of July when they haven't ripened yet. You can make a compote with the pulp by putting it through a food mill (coarse disk), adding sugar and spice to your taste.

Apple Jelly with Vanilla

3⅓ pounds [1.5 kg] green apples
6⅓ cups [1.5 kg/150 cl] water
4⅔ cups [1 kg] granulated sugar
Juice of 1 small lemon
5 vanilla beans

Rinse the apples in cold water. Stem them and cut them in quarters without peeling them. Simmer for 30 minutes on low heat. The apples will be soft.

Collect the juice by pouring the mixture into a fine chinois sieve, pressing the apples lightly with the back of a skimmer. Filter it a second time by pouring it through cheesecloth that you have soaked and wrung out. Let the juice run freely. It's best to let it rest refrigerated overnight.

Next day, measure 4¼ cups [1 kg/1 l] of the juice collected, leaving in the bowl any sediment that has formed overnight. You will have clearer jelly this way. Pour the juice into a preserving pan with the sugar and lemon juice and bring it to a simmer. Skim carefully and add the vanilla beans split lengthwise. Continue cooking on high heat for 5 to 10 minutes, stirring gently. Check the set, and then remove the vanilla beans. Cut them into sticks and distribute them in the jars. Return the mixture to a boil. Put the jelly into the jars immediately and seal.

∼:∼

This jelly is equally delicious flavored with thyme, basil, lemon grass, or rosemary.

Alice's Garden Apple Jelly

3⅓ pounds [1.5 kg] green garden apples
4¼ cups [1.5 kg/150 cl] water
4⅔ cup [1 kg] granulated sugar
Juice of 1 small lemon
Grated zest of ½ lemon

Select very green apples, preferably at the beginning of July, when they are not yet ripe. Rinse the apples in cold water. Remove the stems and cut them in quarters without peeling them. Put them in a preserving pan with water to cover. When this comes to a boil, simmer half an hour on low heat. The apples will be soft to the touch.

Collect the juice by pouring the contents into a fine chinois sieve and pressing on the fruit lightly with the back of the skimmer. Now filter the juice a second time through cheesecloth that has been wet and wrung out. Let the juice run freely. It is best to leave this overnight in a cool place.

Next day, measure 4¼ cups [1 kg/1 l] juice, leaving the sediment that formed overnight in the bottom of the bowl, so the juice will be clearer. Pour the juice into a preserving pan with the sugar, lemon juice, and zest. Bring to a boil and cook for 5 minutes. Skim carefully. Check the set. Put the jelly into jars and seal.

~:~

This jelly is perfect for glazing fruit tarts.

Green Apple and Wild Prune Jelly*

2¼ pounds [1 kg] green apples
8½ cups [2 kg/200 cl/2 l] water
2¼ pounds [1 kg] wild prunes
4⅔ cups [1 kg] granulated sugar
Juice of 1 small lemon

Rinse the apples and the wild prunes in cold water. Remove the stems from the wild prunes. Cut, stem, and core the apples in quarters without peeling them. Put the fruit into a preserving pan and cover it with the water indicated. Bring to a boil and let it simmer for 40 minutes on low heat. The apples will be soft.

Collect the juice by pouring this mixture into a fine chinois sieve and pressing lightly on the fruit with the back of a skimmer. Then filter it a second time by pouring it through a piece of muslin that you have soaked and wrung out. Let the juice run freely. It is preferable to let the juice rest overnight refrigerated.

Next day, measure 4¼ cups [1 kg/1 l] of the juice, leaving in the bottom of the bowl any residue that may have formed overnight. You will have clearer jelly this way. Pour the juice into a preserving pan with the sugar and lemon juice and bring it to a simmer. Skim and continue cooking on high heat for about 10 minutes, stirring gently. Check the set. Put the jelly into jars immediately and seal.

∼:∼

This wild prune jelly has a little taste of bitter almonds

* The wild prune, or prunelle, is the fruit of the wild plum tree. The fruit is small, slate blue, and puckery in flavor. It is often used to make eau-de-vie, and is a member of the plum family.

Apple Jelly with Ceylon Strong Breakfast Tea

3¼ pounds [1.5 kg] green garden apples
4⅔ cups [1 kg] granulated sugar
6½ cups [1.5 kg/150 cl] water *plus* 7 ounces [200 g/20 cl]
Juice of 1 lemon
3½ tablespoons [25 g] Ceylon strong breakfast tea

Rinse the apples in cold water. Remove stems and cut them into quarters without peeling them. Put them in a preserving pan with the water. When it comes to a boil, let it simmer for half an hour on low heat. The apples should be soft to the touch.

Collect the juice by pouring the contents into a chinois sieve, pressing lightly on the fruit with the back of the skimmer. Now filter the juice a second time by pouring it through cheesecloth that has been wet and wrung out. Let the juice run freely. It's best to leave the juice refrigerated overnight.

Next day, measure 4¼ cups [1 kg/1 l] of the juice, leaving the sediment at the bottom of the bowl, for clearer juice. Pour the apple juice into a preserving pan with the sugar and lemon juice. Bring to a boil and cook for 8 minutes. Skim carefully.

Meanwhile, make an infusion with the water and tea: pour the hot water onto the tea and let it steep for 3 minutes. Add the tea to the apple jelly. Return the preparation to a boil. Check the set. Put the jelly into jars immediately and seal.

~:~

You can use teas other than Ceylon strong breakfast. With the apple's sweet taste, many combinations are possible. The important thing is to be careful about the steeping time—otherwise, the tea flavor will be bitter. That is also why the tea is added at the end, so that once the tea has been added, the jelly is boiled just once before it goes into the jars.

Wild Apple Jelly with Cinnamon and Citrus Zest

3⅓ pounds [1.5 kg] wild apples
4⅔ cups [1 kg] granulated sugar
6⅓ cups [1.5 kg/150 cl] water
Zest of ½ lemon
Zest of ½ orange
Juice of 1 small orange
Juice of 1 small lemon
1 cinnamon stick

Rinse the apples in cold water. Remove the stems and cut the fruit into quarters without peeling. Put the fruit into a preserving pan and cover it with the water. Bring it to a boil and let it simmer for half an hour on low heat.

Collect the juice by pouring the contents into a fine chinois sieve and pressing lightly on the fruit with the back of the skimmer. Now filter it a second time by pouring it through cheesecloth that you have wet and wrung out. Let the juice run freely. It is best to leave the juice refrigerated overnight.

Next day, measure 4¼ cups [1 kg/1 l] of the juice, leaving the sediment at the bottom of the bowl, so that the juice will be clearer. Pour the juice into a preserving pan with the sugar, orange juice, orange zest, lemon juice, lemon zest, and the cinnamon stick. Bring to a boil and cook for 5 minutes. Skim carefully.

Check the set. Remove the cinnamon stick. You will use it to decorate the outside of your jars. Put the jelly into jars immediately and seal.

~:~

Wild apples grow at the edges of broad-leaf woods. They should be picked about mid-July before they are ripe.

~:~

This jelly has a more intense fragrance than ordinary orchard apple jelly, and it is more acidic. Still, without spice or citrus flavoring, it is just as delicate.

Alsatian Quetsch Plum

2½ pounds [1.2 kg] Alsatian quetsch plums, *or* 2¼ pounds [1 kg] net
3¾ cups [800 g] granulated sugar
Juice of 2 lemons

Quickly rinse the plums in cold water, dry them in a towel, cut them in half lengthwise to pit them. Combine them with the sugar and lemon juice in a ceramic bowl, and let them macerate an hour. Pour into a preserving pan and bring to a simmer. Return to the bowl. Cover the fruit with a sheet of parchment paper and refrigerate overnight.

Next day, drain the fruit in a fine sieve. Bring the collected syrup to a boil in a preserving pan. Skim and continue cooking on high heat. The syrup will be sufficiently concentrated at 221°F [105°C] on a candy thermometer. Add the plums, bring to a boil on high heat, and continue cooking for about 5 minutes, stirring gently. Skim carefully. Check the set. Put the jam into jars immediately and seal.

~:~

Quetsch plums can be used at various stages of ripeness. It used to be that jam was made with green quetsch plums. For a long time, I used fruit that was barely ripe. Then a friend taught me the best way to use them: for jam, really ripe quetsch plums are best. The flesh is a golden yellow color and has a slight candied taste. This is a fruit that goes beautifully with spices. When we think about Alsatian tarts, what comes to mind is a quetsch plum tart with a light sprinkling of cinnamon sugar.

Pierre Hermé reminded me not long ago that when he was a child he would be in heaven eating fritters filled with plum jam and dusted with cinnamon sugar.

Alsatian Quetsch Plum and Dried Quetsch Plums with Walnuts

2¾ pounds [1.2 kg] Alsatian quetsch plums, to be used dried

2¾ pounds [1.2 kg] Alsatian quetsch plums, *or* 2¼ pounds [1 kg] net,
  to be used fresh

3¾ cups [800 g] granulated sugar

Juice of 1 small lemon

2½ cups [300 g] broken walnut meats

Quickly rinse in cold water the plums that are going to be dried, arrange them on a rack, and put the rack in a 140°F [70°C] oven for about 10 hours. Remove the pits just by pressing on their round "tummies." Chill them; then cut them in half.

Rinse and dry the rest of the plums in a towel. Cut them in half, lengthwise, to pit them. In a ceramic bowl, combine the fresh plums with the sugar, the cut, dried plums, and the lemon juice. Let macerate for an hour, and then pour into a preserving pan. Bring to a boil for 1 minute. Pour back into the bowl. Cover with a sheet of parchment paper and refrigerate overnight.

Next day, bring this preparation to a boil and continue cooking on high heat for about 5 minutes, stirring gently. Skim carefully. Add the broken walnuts. Return to a boil. Check the set. Put the jam into jars and seal.

Alsatian Quetsch Plum and Mirabelle Plum with Cinnamon

1⅓ pounds [600 g] Alsatian quetsch plums, *or* 1 pound 2 ounces [500 g] net
1⅓ pounds [600 g] Nancy mirabelle plums, *or* 1 pound 2 ounces [500 g] net
3¾ cups [800 g] granulated sugar
Juice of 1 small lemon
2 cinnamon sticks

Quickly rinse the quetsch and mirabelle plums in cold water. Dry them in a towel and cut them in half lengthwise to remove the pits.

In a ceramic bowl, mix the cut fruit with the sugar, lemon juice, and cinnamon sticks. After an hour of maceration, pour the contents into a preserving pan and bring to a boil for 1 minute. Pour back into the bowl. Cover with a sheet of parchment paper and refrigerate overnight.

Next day, bring this preparation to a boil and continue cooking on high heat for about 5 minutes, stirring gently. Skim carefully, return to a boil, and remove the cinnamon sticks. Check the set. Put the jam into jars immediately and seal.

Alsatian Quetsch Plum
with Elderberries and Floral Honey

2¾ pounds [1.2 kg] Alsatian quetsch plums, *or* 2¼ pounds [1 kg] net
9 ounces (*about 2 ½ cups*) [250 g] elderberries
3¾ cups [800 g] granulated sugar
Juice of 1 small lemon
7 ounces [200 g] floral honey

Quickly rinse the plums in cold water, dry them in a towel, and split them lengthwise to remove the pits.

Rinse the elderberry bunches before stripping off the berries. In a ceramic bowl, combine the pitted plums, elderberries, sugar, honey, and lemon juice. Let macerate for an hour, and then pour into a preserving pan and bring to a boil for a minute. Pour back into the bowl. Cover with a sheet of parchment paper and refrigerate overnight.

Next day, bring this preparation to a boil, continue cooking on high heat for about 5 minutes, stirring gently, and then skim carefully. Return to a boil. Check the set. Put the jam into jars immediately and seal.

Alsatian Quetsch Plum and Apple with Anise and Vanilla

1⅓ pounds [600 g] Alsatian quetsch plums, *or* 1¼ pounds [500 g] net

1¾ pounds [750 g] apples, *or* 1¼ pounds [500 g] net

3¾ cups [800 g] granulated sugar

Juice of 1 small lemon

1 star anise

2 vanilla beans

Quickly rinse the plums in cold water, dry them in a towel, and cut them in half lengthwise to remove the pits.

Peel the apples, core them, and slice them thin. In a ceramic bowl, combine the prepared fruit with the sugar, lemon juice, star anise, and vanilla beans split lengthwise in a bowl. Let macerate an hour, and then pour into a preserving pan, bring to a boil, and cook for 1 minute. Pour back into the bowl. Cover with a sheet of parchment paper and refrigerate overnight.

Next day, bring to a boil and continue cooking on high heat for about 5 minutes, stirring gently. Skim carefully. Remove the vanilla beans and star anise. Return to a boil. Check the set. Put the jam into jars immediately and seal.

~:~

You can decorate each jar with a little piece of a vanilla bean and a point of star anise.

L'Alsacienne

2¾ pounds [1.2 kg] Alsatian quetsch plums, *or* 2¼ pounds [1 kg] net
1¼ cups [300 g/30 cl] Alsatian Pinot Noir
4⅔ cups [1 kg] granulated sugar
Juice of 1 small lemon
1 vanilla bean

Quickly rinse the plums in cold water, dry them in a towel, and split them lengthwise to remove the pits. In a ceramic bowl, combine the prepared fruit with the sugar, lemon juice, and the vanilla bean, split lengthwise. Let macerate for an hour, and then pour into a preserving pan and bring to a boil for a minute. Pour back into the bowl. Cover with a sheet of parchment paper and refrigerate overnight.

Next day, bring to a boil again and continue cooking on high heat for about 5 minutes, stirring gently. Skim carefully, and add the Pinot Noir. Return to a boil for about 5 minutes, stirring gently.

Skim again if needed, and remove the vanilla beans. Return to a boil. Check the set. Put the jam into jars immediately and seal.

Greengage Plum

2¾ pounds [1.2 kg] greengage plums, *or* 2¼ pounds [1 kg] net
3¾ cups [800 g] granulated sugar
Juice of 1 small lemon

Rinse the greengage plums, dry them in a towel, and split them lengthwise to remove the pits. In a ceramic bowl, combine the fruit with the sugar and lemon juice. After an hour's maceration, bring this preparation to a simmer. Now pour back into a bowl. Cover with a sheet of parchment paper and refrigerate overnight.

Next day, pour this mixture into a fine sieve. Bring the collected syrup to a boil in a preserving pan. Skim and continue cooking on high heat. The syrup will be sufficiently concentrated at 221°F [105°C] on candy thermometer. Add the greengage plums and return to a boil, cooking on high heat for about 5 minutes, stirring gently. Skim carefully. Check the set. Put the jam into jars immediately and seal.

Greengage Plum with Vanilla and Dried Lemon Slices

2¾ pounds [1.2 kg] greengage plums, *or* 2¼ pounds [1 kg] net

3¾ cups [850 g] granulated sugar

Juice of 3 small lemons

3 lemons

2 vanilla beans

To make the dried lemon slices, wash the lemons, scrubbing them with a brush, and slice them into rounds. Place the rounds on a rack and dry them in a 125–140°F [50–60°C] oven for about 8 hours.

Rinse the greengage plums, dry them in a towel, and split them lengthwise to remove the pits. Combine them with the sugar and lemon juice in a ceramic bowl. After 1 hour of maceration, pour them into a preserving pan and bring the contents to a boil for 1 minute. Pour back into the bowl. Cover with a sheet of parchment paper and refrigerate overnight.

Next day, bring this preparation to a boil with the vanilla beans, split lengthwise, and the dried lemon slices cut into small pieces. Continue cooking on high heat for about 5 minutes, stirring gently. Skim carefully and return to a boil. Check the set. Put the jam into jars immediately and seal.

Greengage and Mirabelle Plums with Mint

1⅓ pounds [600 g] greengage plums, *or* 1 pound 2 ounces [500 g] net
1⅓ pounds [600 g] mirabelle plums, *or* 1 pound 2 ounces [500 g] net
3¾ cups [800 g] granulated sugar
Juice of 1 small lemon
25 leaves of fresh mint

Rinse the greengage and mirabelle plums in cold water. Dry them in a towel and halve them to remove the stones. In a bowl, combine the fruit, sugar, and lemon juice. Let the preparation macerate for 1 hour.

Bring the mixture to a boil in a preserving pan, and then turn it into a bowl. Cover with a piece of parchment paper, and refrigerate it overnight.

Next day, bring the mixture to a boil in the preserving pan, skim, and continue cooking on high heat for about 5 minutes, stirring gently. Add the mint leaves and return to a boil. Check the set. Put the jam into jars immediately and seal.

Elderberry Jelly

---

4 pounds [1.8 kg] **elderberries**
4⅔ cups [1 kg] **granulated sugar**
7 ounces [200 g/20 cl] **water**
Juice of 1 small lemon

Rinse the elderberry bunches in cold water, drain them, and remove the berries from the stems. Put the berries into a preserving pan and bring them to a boil with the water. Cover the pan and let the berries soften on low heat for 5 minutes.

Collect the juice by pouring this preparation into a fine chinois sieve and pressing the fruit with the back of the skimmer. Filter the juice by pouring it through cheesecloth that has been wet and wrung out. Pour the juice (4¾ cups [1.1 kg/110 cl]) into a preserving pan with the lemon juice and sugar. Bring to a boil and cook for 10 minutes. Skim carefully. Return to a boil. Check the set. Put the jelly into jars immediately and seal.

~:~

To make this jelly successfully, you have to pick the elderberries when they are quite dark but still firm.

~:~

You can reduce the sugar in this recipe, but then you'll have to cook it longer. Your jelly will have a slightly bitter and caramelized taste.

Fall

Dried Fruit and Honey

2¼ pounds [1 kg] Ida Red apples,* *or* 1¾ pounds [800 g] net
2½ cups [500 g] granulated sugar
3½ ounces [100 g] pine honey
3½ ounces [100 g/10 cl] water
3½ ounces [100 g] Smyrna raisins
3½ ounces [100 g] candied orange rind, diced small
3½ ounces [100 g] broken walnut meats
3½ ounces [100 g] small blanched almonds
3½ ounces [100 g] pine nuts
3½ ounces [100 g] skinned pistachios
Juice and finely grated zest of 1 lemon
Juice and finely grated zest of 1 orange

Peel the apples, halve them, core them, and cut them into small cubes. In a preserving pan, combine the apples, grapes, diced candied orange rind, and the zest and juice of the lemon and the orange. Cover with a piece of parchment paper and let macerate 1 hour.

In a preserving pan, bring the sugar, honey, and water to a boil. Continue cooking. The sugar syrup will concentrate sufficiently at 240°F [115°C] on a candy thermometer. Add the macerated diced apples, grapes, and diced candied orange peel. Bring the mixture to a boil, stirring gently; skim and continue cooking on high heat for about 5 minutes, continuing to stir. Check the set. Add the dried ingredients (almonds, walnuts, pine nuts, and pistachios) and return to a boil. Put the jam in jars immediately and seal.

* Ida Red apples are large, bright red apples with firm, crisp, and slightly acidic white flesh.

Dried Fruit, Apple Slices, and Fresh Walnuts*

2¾ pounds [1.2 kg] apples, *or* 2¼ pounds [1 kg] net

2¾ cups [600 g] granulated sugar

Juice of 2 small lemons

3½ ounces [100 g/10 cl] water

11 ounces [300 g] very soft, dried apricots

11 ounces [300 g] very soft, dried figs

3½ ounces [100 g] fresh walnut meats

7 ounces [200 g] Green Apple Jelly (*page 120*)

⅛ teaspoon [pinch] ground cinnamon

Peel the apples. Remove stems, core, and cut each apple into eight wedges.

In a preserving pan, combine the apples, sugar, water, and lemon juice. Bring this preparation to a simmer. Pour it into a ceramic bowl. Cover the fruit with a sheet of parchment paper and refrigerate overnight.

Next day, repeat this procedure.

The third day, break the walnut meats and remove their skin. Bring the apple preparation to a boil

*"Fresh" here means freshly picked, not having been subjected to a long drying period as the walnuts purchased in supermarkets "Fresh" nuts can be found at farmers' markets, called "new crop."

again, adding the apple jelly, the dried fruit cut into julienne $\frac{1}{16}$ inch [1 mm] wide, and the cinnamon. Return to a boil, skim, and continue cooking on high heat, stirring gently for about 10 minutes. Skim again if needed. Add the fresh walnuts. Return to a boil. Check the set. Put the jam into jars immediately and seal.

∾:∾

If you are not able to find soft enough figs and apricots, you can soak the dried fruit that is available in cold water for 12 hours to rehydrate it, changing the water two or three times during the day.

Spiced Beer Jelly

---

3 cups 2 ounces [750 g/75 cl] dark beer
1¾ pounds [750 g] Granny Smith apples
3 cups 2 ounces [750 g/75 cl] water
5¼ cups [1.15 kg] granulated sugar
Juice of 1 small lemon
Zest of 1 orange finely grated
2 sticks of cinnamon
¼ teaspoon [2 pinches] ground cardamom

Rinse the apples in cold water. Stem, core, and cut the apples into quarters without peeling them. Put the fruit in a preserving pan and cover them with the water. Bring to a boil and allow to simmer for 30 minutes on low heat. The apples will be soft. Collect the juice by pouring this preparation into a fine chinois strainer, pressing lightly on the fruit with the back of a skimmer. Then filter the juice a second time by pouring it through cheesecloth that you have soaked and wrung out. Let the juice run freely. It is preferable to let the juice rest overnight in the refrigerator.

Next day, measure 2 cups 1 ounce [500 g] of the juice, leaving in the bottom of the bowl any residue that settled out overnight. You will have clearer jelly this way. Pour the apple juice, beer, sugar, orange zest, lemon juice, cinnamon sticks, and ground cardamom into the preserving pan and bring it to a simmer. Skim carefully. Continue cooking on high heat for 10 to 15 minutes, stirring gently. Skim again if necessary. Check the set. Remove the cinnamon sticks and return to a boil. Put the jelly in jars immediately and seal.

Chestnut with Vanilla

2¾ pounds [1.2 kg] chestnuts, *or* 1¾ pounds [800 g] net
4⅔ cups [1 kg] granulated sugar
1¾ cup [400 g/40 cl] water
1 vanilla bean

Make a deep cut in each chestnut with the point of a knife to cut through its two skins. Put chestnuts in boiling water. After 3 minutes, you will be able to remove the outer shell and the inner skin. Chestnuts can be easily peeled if they don't cool off. If they do get cold, the second skin will be difficult to remove.

In a preserving pan, combine the chestnuts, sugar, water, and vanilla bean, split lengthwise. Bring to a boil and cook for about 15 minutes, stirring gently. The chestnuts will be soft. Pour the mixture into a ceramic bowl. Cover with a sheet of parchment paper and refrigerate overnight.

Next day, bring this preparation to a boil, stirring constantly. Skim if need be. Remove the vanilla bean. Crush the large pieces of chestnut with a wooden spoon. Continue cooking on low heat for about 10 minutes, stirring continuously. Remove the vanilla bean and put a bit of it into each jar. Return to a boil. Check the set. Put the jam into jars immediately and seal.

Chestnut and Fresh Walnut*

2¾ pounds [1.2 kg] chestnuts, *or* 1¾ pounds [800 g] net
4⅔ cups [1 kg] granulated sugar
1¾ cups [400 g/40 cl] water
3½ ounces (*1 scant cup*) [100 g] fresh walnut meats
1 vanilla bean

Make a deep cut in each chestnut with the point of a knife to cut through its two skins. Put chestnuts in boiling water. After 3 minutes, you will be able to remove the outer shell and the inner skin. Chestnuts can be easily peeled if they don't cool off. If they do get cold, the second skin will be difficult to remove.

In a preserving pan combine the chestnuts, the sugar, water, and vanilla bean split lengthwise. Bring to a boil and cook for about 15 minutes, stirring gently. The chestnuts will be soft. Pour into a ceramic bowl. Cover with a sheet of parchment paper and refrigerate overnight.

Next day, break the fresh walnuts and remove their skins. Bring the chestnut preparation to a boil, stirring continuously. Skim, if necessary. Remove the vanilla bean. Crush the large pieces of chestnut with a wooden spoon or a mixer. Add the walnuts. Keep cooking on low heat for about 10 minutes. Skim if needed. Divide the vanilla bean among the jars. Bring the jam to a boil again. Check the set. Put the jam into jars immediately and seal.

* *"Fresh" here means freshly picked, not having been subjected to a long drying period as the walnuts purchased in supermarkets "Fresh" nuts can be found at farmers' markets, called "new crop."*

Chestnut and William Pear with Vanilla

2¾ pounds [1.2 kg] chestnuts, *or* 1¾ pounds [800 g] net

2¾ pounds [1.2 kg] ripe but still firm William or Bartlett pears,
    or 2¼ pounds [1 kg] net

4⅔ cups [1 kg] granulated sugar *plus* 3¾ cups [800 g]

1¾ cups [400 g/40 cl] water

Juice of 1 small lemon

2 vanilla beans

Make a deep cut in each chestnut with the point of a knife to cut through its two skins. Put chestnuts in boiling water. After 3 minutes, you will be able to remove the outer shell and the inner skin. Chestnuts can be easily peeled if they don't cool off. If they do get cold, the second skin will be difficult to remove.

In a preserving pan, combine the chestnuts, 4⅔ cups [1 kg/1 l] sugar, water, and 1 vanilla bean, split lengthwise. Bring to a boil, and cook for about 15 minutes, stirring gently. The chestnuts will be soft. Pour into a ceramic bowl. Cover with a sheet of parchment paper and refrigerate overnight.

Peel the pears, core them, and cut them into small dice. In a preserving pan, combine the pears, 3¾ cups [800 g] sugar, lemon juice, and the second vanilla bean, split lengthwise. Bring this preparation to a simmer. Pour it into a bowl and cover the fruit with a sheet of parchment paper. Refrigerate overnight.

Next day, put the chestnuts through a food mill (fine disk). Bring the two preparations to a boil in separate preserving pans, stirring gently. Skim if need be. Continue cooking each on high heat for about 5 minutes, stirring continuously. Remove the vanilla beans. Combine the two jams in the same pan. Return to a boil and continue cooking on low heat for about 5 minutes. Skim again if needed. Check the set. Put the jam into jars immediately and seal.

Cider Jelly with Vanilla

---

3 cups 2 ounces [750 g/75 cl] cider
1¾ pounds [750 g] Granny Smith apples
3 cups 2 ounces [750 g/75 cl] water
5¼ cups [1.15 kg] sugar
Juice of 1 small lemon
3 vanilla beans

Rinse the apples in cold water. Stem and core the apples and cut them in quarters without peeling them. Put the fruit into a preserving pan and cover with the water. Bring to a boil and allow to simmer for 30 minutes on low heat. The apples will be soft.

Collect the juice by pouring this preparation into a fine chinois sieve, pressing lightly on the fruit with the back of a skimmer. Filter it a second time through cheesecloth you have soaked and wrung out. Let the juice run freely. It is preferable to let it rest overnight refrigerated.

Next day, measure 2 cups 1 ounce [500 g/50 cl] of the juice, leaving in the bottom of the bowl any residue that has settled out overnight. You will have clearer jelly this way. Pour the apple juice, cider, sugar, and lemon juice into a preserving pan and bring to a simmer. Skim carefully. Add the vanilla beans split lengthwise. Continue cooking on high heat for 10 to 15 minutes, stirring gently. Skim again if necessary. Check the set, remove the vanilla beans, and return to a boil. Put the jelly into jars immediately and seal.

You can cut the vanilla beans into little sticks and use them to decorate the outside of the jars.

Quince Juice

Select apple quinces or pear quinces that are ripe and very fragrant. Wipe the quinces with a towel to remove their fine fuzz.

Wash them in cold water, and remove the stems and any remaining blossom. Cut them in quarters.

Put the quince quarters into a preserving pan and cover them with water. Bring to a boil and simmer on low heat for an hour, stirring occasionally. Collect the juice by pouring the preparation into a fine chinois sieve and pressing the fruit lightly with the back of the skimmer. Now filter it a second time by pouring it through cheesecloth that has been wet and wrung out. Let the juice run freely.

I advise you to leave the juice overnight refrigerated. For clear, shining jelly, carefully decant the juice, leaving the solids behind, before using it.

∼:∼

This juice is an ingredient in a number of recipes for quince jams and jellies. You can pour it into small containers and keep it in the freezer.

∼:∼

You can make a compote with the pulp left over by putting it through a food mill, sweetening it with sugar, and spicing it with cardamom and cinnamon and some orange or lemon peel.

Quince Jelly

4¼ cups [1 kg/1 l] quince juice
4⅓ cups [950 g] granulated sugar
Juice of 1 small lemon

Put the quince juice, sugar, and lemon juice into a preserving pan. Bring to a boil, skim, and continue cooking on high heat for about 10 minutes. Skim again if need be. Check the set and return to a boil. Put the jelly into jars immediately and seal.

Spiced Quince Jelly

4¼ cups [1 kg/1 l] quince juice

4⅓ cups [950 g] granulated sugar

⅛ teaspoon [pinch] finely grated lemon zest

¼ teaspoon [2 pinches] finely grated orange zest

Juice of 1 small lemon

1 clove

⅛ teaspoon [pinch] cinnamon

⅛ teaspoon [pinch] gingerbread spices*

⅛ teaspoon [pinch] fresh grated ginger

Put the quince juice, sugar, lemon juice, lemon, and orange zests and spices into a preserving pan. Bring to a boil, skim and continue cooking on high heat 10 minutes. Skim again if need be. Check the set. Return to a boil. Put the jelly in jars immediately and seal.

* Épices à pain d'épices, or gingerbread spice, is a blend of spices in which anise predominates, plus cinnamon and cloves. Apple pie spice can be used, with a pinch of anise.

Quince, Orange, and Cardamom

A scant 3 pounds [1.3 kg] apple quince or pear quince, *or* 1¾ pounds [800 g] net
7 ounces [200 g/20 cl] quince juice
4 cups [850 g] granulated sugar *plus* ½ cup [100 g]
2 oranges
Juice of 1 small lemon
Juice of 2 small oranges
⅛ teaspoon [pinch] ground cardamom

Wipe the quinces with a towel to remove their slight fuzz. Rinse them in cold water, peel them, and remove the stem, remaining blossom, and hard parts. Cut them in four and remove the core and seeds. Cut them into sections, and then in thin slices. (Cores, skins, and seeds may be used to make quince juice.) Rinse and brush the oranges in cold water and slice them in very thin rounds.

In a preserving pan poach the orange slices with ½ cup [100 g] sugar and the orange juice. Keep cooking at a boil until the rounds are translucent. Add the quince slices, quince juice, lemon juice, 4 cups [850 g] sugar, and cardamom. Bring to a simmer and pour into a ceramic bowl. Cover with a sheet of parchment paper and refrigerate overnight.

Next day, bring the preparation to a boil, skim, and continue cooking on high heat for about 10 minutes, stirring gently. Skim again if needed and return to a boil. Check the set. Put the jam into jars and seal.

Quince with Christmas Flavors

A scant 3 pounds [1.3 kg] apple quince or pear quince, *or* 1¾ pounds [800 g] net
15 ounces [400 g/40 cl] quince juice
5 cups [1.1 kg] granulated sugar
Juice of 1 small orange
⅜ teaspoon [3 pinches] finely grated lemon rind
Juice of 1 small lemon
⅜ teaspoon [3 pinches] finely grated orange rind
¼ teaspoon [2 pinches] gingerbread spices*

Wipe the quinces with a towel to remove their slight fuzz. Wash them in cold water. Peel them. Remove their stems, any remaining blossoms, and hard parts. Cut them in four, and remove the core and the seeds. Cut the quarters into fine dice. (Cores, skins, and seeds can be used to make quince juice.)

In a preserving pan, combine the diced quince, quince juice, juice and zest of the orange and the lemon, spices, and sugar. Bring to a simmer. Pour into a bowl. Cover with a sheet of parchment paper and refrigerate overnight.

Next day, bring this mixture to a boil in a preserving pan. Skim and continue cooking on high heat for about 10 minutes, stirring gently. Skim again if necessary. Return to a boil. Check the set. Put the jam into jars and seal.

* Épices à pain d'épices, *or gingerbread spice, is a blend of spices in which anise predominates, plus cinnamon and cloves. Apple pie spice can be used, with a pinch of anise.*

Quince with Orange Blossom Honey

A scant 3 pounds [1.3 kg] apple quince or pear quince, *or* 1¾ pounds [800 g] net
1¼ cups [300 g/30 cl] quince juice
2¾ cups [600 g] granulated sugar
1½ cups [350 g] orange blossom honey
Zest of 1 orange
Juice of 1 lemon

Wipe the quince with a towel to remove their slight fuzz. Rinse them in cold water, peel them, and remove the stem, any remaining blossoms, and hard parts. Cut them in quarters, remove the center and the seeds, and cut the quarters into julienne. (Cores, skin, and seeds can be used to make quince juice.)

In a preserving pan, combine the julienned quince with sugar, orange blossom honey, orange zest, lemon juice, and the quince juice. Bring to a simmer and pour into a ceramic bowl. Cover with a sheet of parchment paper and refrigerate overnight.

Next day, bring this preparation to a boil in a preserving pan. Skim and keep cooking on high heat for about 10 minutes, stirring gently. Skim if need be and return to a boil. Check the set. Put the jam into jars and seal.

Quince with Fresh and Preserved Ginger

2¼ pounds [1 kg] apple quince or pear quince, *or* 1⅓ pounds [600 kg] net
2½ cups [600 g/60 cl] quince juice
3¼ cups [700 g] sugar
Juice of 1 small lemon
3½ ounces [100 g] candied ginger, diced small
1¾ ounces [50 g] grated fresh ginger

Wipe the quinces with a towel to remove their fine fuzz. Rinse them in cold water, peel them, and remove the stems and what remains of the blossom and hard parts. Cut them into eight sections, removing the core and seeds. (Cores, skin, and seeds can be used to make quince juice.)

In a preserving pan combine the quince sections, sugar, fresh grated ginger, quince juice, and lemon juice. Bring to a boil and continue cooking on low heat for 10 minutes. Skim carefully. The quince pieces will be soft. Stir to mix. Add the preserved ginger. Return to a boil, stirring gently. Skim again if necessary. Continue cooking on high heat about 5 minutes, stirring continuously. Check the set. Put the jam into jars immediately and seal.

Quince with Nostradamus Spices

A scant 3 pounds [1.3 kg] quince, *or* 1¾ pounds [800 g] net

1¼ cups [300 g/30 cl] quince juice

4¼ cups [900 g] granulated sugar

Juice of 2 small lemons

2 whole cloves

¼ teaspoon [2 pinches] ground cinnamon

⅛ teaspoon [pinch] ground cardamom

Wipe the quinces with a towel to remove their slight fuzz. Wash them in cold water. Peel them, and remove the stem and any remaining blossom and hard parts. Cut them in quarters, removing the center and the seeds. Cut each quarter in two lengthwise, or in three depending on the size of the fruit. (Cores, skins and seeds can be used to make quince juice.)

In a preserving pan, combine the quince pieces with the sugar, lemon juice, quince juice, and the spices and bring to a simmer. Simmer for 2 minutes, and pour into a ceramic bowl. Cover the fruit with a sheet of parchment paper. Refrigerate overnight.

Repeat this procedure four days in a row. The fifth day, bring the preparation to a boil in a preserving pan, skim carefully, and continue cooking about 10 minutes on low heat, stirring gently. Lift out the quince pieces with the skimmer and distribute them among the jars. Return the spiced jelly to a final boil. Check the set. Finish filling the jars. Seal.

~:~

The quince is the last fruit of the autumn harvest and my favorite! It doesn't have an appealing appearance, but as soon as it's cooked, it takes on the color of gold and releases a magic fragrance that reminds me of the scents of Christmas.

~:~

Always be careful to pick quinces ripe before they get spotted. For jelly, apple quince are preferable because they have more pectin. Pear quince, sometimes a little softer, are better for making purées or jellies that have bits of fruit in them to give them texture.

~:~

In times gone by, quince was thought to be medicinal. Nostradamus, astrologer and physician, handed down a jam-making treatise that includes a wonderful quince recipe.

Andrée's Orchard Quince Jam

2¼ pounds [1 kg] apple or pear quince, *or* 1⅓ pounds [600 g] net
2 cups 1 ounce [500 g/50 cl] quince juice
4 cups [850 g] granulated sugar
Juice of 1 small lemon

Wipe the quince with a towel to remove their slight fuzz. Wash them in cold water. Peel them, and remove the stem, any remaining blossoms, and hard parts. Cut them in 8 sections, removing the center and the seeds. (Center, skin, and seeds can be used to make quince juice.)

In a preserving pan combine the quince pieces, sugar, lemon juice, and quince juice. Bring to a boil and cook on low heat for about 10 minutes. Skim carefully. The quince will be soft. Stir the jam to mix it. Return the jam to a boil, stirring gently. Skim again if need be and continue cooking on high heat for about 5 minutes, stirring constantly. Check the set. Put the jam in jars immediately and seal.

My Father's Jam

2¼ pounds [1 kg] apple or pear quince, *or* 1⅓ pounds [600 g] net
7 ounces [200 g/20 cl] quince juice
12 ounces [300 g] raspberries, *or* 9 ounces [250 g] raspberry pulp
4¼ cups [900 g] granulated sugar
Juice of 1 small lemon
1½ tablespoons [20 g/2 cl] kirsch

Wipe the quince with a towel to remove their slight fuzz. Wash them in cold water. Peel them, and remove the stem, any remaining blossoms, and hard parts. Cut them into quarters, and remove the center and the seeds. Cut them into very thin slices. (Cores, skins, and seeds can be used to make quince juice.)

Pick over the raspberries and put them through a food mill (fine disk).

In a preserving pan, combine the quince, sugar, lemon juice, quince juice, and raspberry pulp. Bring to a boil. Skim and continue cooking on high heat for 10 to 15 minutes, stirring gently. Skim again if necessary. Return to a boil. Check the set. Off heat, add the kirsch. Stir to mix. Put the jam into jars immediately and seal.

Rose Hips

There are two ways to make rose hip purée:

First Method

Rose hips must be picked in the fall. They'll have turned a dark red by then.

Rinse them quickly in cold water and remove their stems and caps. Cut them in two, lengthwise, and remove seeds and hair. Rinse the emptied hips. Now put them in a saucepan with water to cover.

Bring to a boil and simmer about half an hour, stirring occasionally. When they cool, put the hips and the remaining cooking water through a food mill (fine disk) to separate the skins.

Second Method

Pick the rose hips. Rinse them quickly in cold water and remove the stems and caps.

Put them in a saucepan with water to cover. Bring to a boil and let simmer for half an hour, stirring occasionally. When the rose hips cool, put them through a food mill several times, using a finer disk each time. This method separates the seeds and hair.

To complete the procedure, work the pulp through a sieve to catch the last remaining hairs.

Rose Hip with Vanilla

2¼ pounds (*about 4½ cups*) [1 kg] rose hip pulp
3¾ cups [800 g] granulated sugar
Juice of 1 small lemon
1 vanilla bean

In a preserving pan, combine the rose hip pulp, lemon juice, vanilla bean, split lengthwise, and the sugar. Bring to a boil, stirring continuously. Skim if needed. Continue cooking for 5 minutes, stirring the entire time. Remove the vanilla bean, which will be used to decorate the jars. Check the set. Put the jam into jars immediately and seal.

~:~

This jam has an incomparably silky texture. It brings to mind a dessert that I have enjoyed so much: a small fritter filled with rose hip jam. Try this, and have with it an Alsatian muscatel, made from noble grapes.

Rose Hip with Orange

2¼ pounds (*about 4½ cups*) [1 kg] rose hip pulp

3¾ cups [800 g] granulated sugar *plus* 1 cup [200 g]

2 oranges

Juice of 2 small oranges

Juice of 1 lemon

Rinse the oranges and scrub them with a brush in cold water. Cut them into very thin rounds. In a preserving pan, poach the orange slices with 1 cup [200 g] sugar and the orange juice. Cook until the slices are translucent. Add the rose hip pulp, lemon juice, and 3¾ cups [800 g] sugar.

Bring to a boil, stirring constantly. Skim if needed. Continue cooking for 5 minutes, stirring the entire time. Check the set. Put the jams into jars immediately and seal.

*The primordial
marriage: fruit
and sugar*

Apple with Caramel
(page 195)

Pear with Pinot Noir
and Cinnamon
(page 183)

Fig and Pear (page 165)

Gewürztraminer Wine Jelly (page 206), Alsatian Muscat Grape Jelly (page 171)

Dried Fruit and Honey
(page 141)

Pear Sections with Balsamic Vinegar and Spices (pages 190–91), My Grandmother's Pear Jam (page 188), Pears with Glaceéd Chestnuts (page 185)

*Vineyard Peach
and Raspberry
with Cardamom
(page 177)*

Fig with Vanilla

2¼ pounds [1 kg] fresh Bourjasotte* figs
3¾ cups [800 g] granulated sugar
Juice of 1 small lemon
2 vanilla beans

Select small black figs. Rinse them in cold water and dry them in a towel. Remove the stems. Slice them. In a bowl, combine the fruit, sugar, lemon juice, and vanilla beans, split lengthwise. Cover with a sheet of parchment paper and let macerate 1 hour.

Pour this preparation into a preserving pan and bring to a simmer. Pour back into the bowl. Cover with a sheet of parchment paper and refrigerate overnight.

Next day, bring this preparation to a boil in a preserving pan. Skim and continue cooking on high heat for 5 to 10 minutes, stirring gently. Remove the vanilla beans and use them to decorate the jars. Return to a boil. Check the set. Put the jam into jars and seal.

∾∶∾

As a child, I wasn't acquainted with fresh figs. They were used very seldom in Alsatian pastry making, because they were very rarely found in our orchards. One day Alain Ducasse introduced me to his favorite dessert: the marvelous Bellone figs, half-cooked in a sugar syrup with vanilla and served with thick crème fraiche. I became a believer!*

*Bourjasotte figs are purple skinned with deep red flesh and rich-flavored syrupy juice. Bellone figs are large and purple skinned with red pulp, quite sweet, in season from July to October.

Fig, Orange, and Walnut

2¼ pounds [1 kg] fresh Bourjasotte figs
3¾ cups [800 g] granulated sugar *plus* ½ cup [100 g]
2 oranges
Juice of 2 small oranges
5 ounces [150 g] broken walnut meats
Juice of 1 lemon

Rinse and scrub the oranges with a brush in cold water and slice them in very thin rounds. Select small black figs. Rinse them in cold water as well and dry them with a towel. Remove the stems. Cut the figs in slices. In a ceramic bowl, combine the figs, 3¾ cups [800 g] sugar, and lemon juice. Let this macerate an hour.

In a preserving pan, poach the orange slices with the orange juice and ½ cup [100 g] sugar. Continue cooking until the slices are translucent. Add the macerated figs. Bring this preparation to a simmer. Pour it back into a bowl. Cover with a sheet of parchment paper and refrigerate overnight.

Next day, bring the preparation to a boil in a preserving pan. Skim and cook on high heat for 5 to 10 minutes, stirring gently. Add the broken walnuts and return to a boil. Check the set. Put the jam into jars and seal.

Fig and Pear

1¾ pounds [800 g] fresh figs
1 pound [400 g] William or Bartlett pears, ripe but still firm,
   or ¾ pounds [300 g] net
4⅔ cups [1 kg] granulated sugar
Juice of 1 small lemon

Select small white figs. Rinse them in cold water and dry them with a towel. Remove the stems. Cut the fruit in slices. Peel the pears, core them, and cut them in dice. In a ceramic bowl, combine the figs, diced pears, sugar, and lemon juice. Cover with a sheet of parchment paper and allow to macerate for an hour.

Pour the mixture into a preserving pan. Bring to a simmer. Pour back into a bowl. Cover with a sheet of parchment paper and refrigerate overnight.

Next day, bring the mixture to a boil in a preserving pan. Skim and continue cooking on high heat 5 to 10 minutes, mixing gently. Check the set. Put the jam into jars immediately and seal.

Fig and Gewürztraminer with Pine Nuts

1¾ pounds [800 g] Bourjasotte figs

3¾ cups [800 g] sugar

7 ounces [200 g/20 cl] Gewürztraminer

Juice of 1 small lemon

3½ ounces [100 g] pine nuts

Choose small black figs. Rinse them in cold water and dry them in a towel. Remove the stems and cut the fruit into thin slices. In a bowl, combine the figs, sugar, Gewürztraminer, and lemon juice. Cover the bowl with a piece of parchment paper and let the fruit macerate 30 minutes.

Turn this mixture into a preserving pan and bring to a simmer. Pour it into a bowl, cover it with a piece of parchment paper, and refrigerate overnight.

Next day, bring the mixture to a boil in a preserving pan, skim, and continue cooking on high heat for about 5 minutes, stirring gently. Check the set. Add the pine nuts and return to a boil. Put the jam into jars immediately and seal.

Fig and Honey with Bay

2¼ pounds [1 kg] Bourjasotte figs
3¼ cups [700 g] sugar
3½ ounces [100 g] floral honey
6 bay leaves
Juice of 1 small lemon

Choose small black figs. Rinse them in cold water and dry them in a towel. Remove the stems and cut the fruit into thin slices. In a bowl combine the figs, sugar, honey, lemon juice, and bay leaves. Cover the bowl with a piece of parchment paper and let the fruit macerate for 30 minutes.

Pour this mixture into a preserving pan and bring to a simmer. Turn into a bowl, cover with a piece of parchment paper, and refrigerate overnight.

Next day, bring the mixture to a boil and continue cooking on high heat for about 5 minutes, stirring gently. Check the set. Remove the bay leaves and return to a boil. Put the jam into jars immediately and seal.

New Year's Jam

1⅓ pounds [600 g] fresh figs

1 pound 2 ounces [500 g] soft, dried figs

2 cups 1 ounce [500 g/50 cl] orange juice

2¾ cups [600 g] granulated sugar

¼ teaspoon [2 pinches] finely grated lemon zest

¼ teaspoon [2 pinches] finely grated orange zest

⅛ teaspoon [pinch] ground cinnamon

⅛ teaspoon [pinch] ground cardamom

⅛ teaspoon [pinch] ground star anise

Juice of 1 small lemon

Select small black figs. Rinse them in cold water and dry them with a towel. Remove the stems. Cut the fruit in slices. Cut off the stems of the dried figs and trim them into sticks a little less than ½ inch [1 cm] wide.

In a preserving pan, bring the fresh figs, the orange and lemon juices, and sugar to a boil. Pour this into a bowl. Cover with a sheet of parchment paper and refrigerate overnight.

Next day, bring to a boil. Skim. Add the orange and lemon zest, cinnamon, cardamom, and star anise. Continue cooking on high for about 10 minutes, stirring gently. Skim again if needed. Return to a boil. Check the set. Put the jam in jars immediately and seal.

Alsatian Muscat Grape

A scant 3 pounds [1.3 kg] Alsatian muscat grapes, *or* 2¼ pounds [1 kg] net
3¾ cups [800 g] sugar
Juice of 1 small lemon
7 ounces [200 g] **Green Apple Jelly** (*page 120*)

Choose the very fragrant Ottonel muscat grapes. Rinse them in cold water and drain them by putting them in a towel. Stem them. In a bowl, combine the muscat grapes, sugar, and lemon juice, and let the fruit macerate for 10 minutes. In a preserving pan, bring this preparation to a simmer. Turn the mixture into a bowl, cover it with a piece of parchment paper, and refrigerate overnight.

Next day, pour the mixture into a sieve, pressing the grapes with the fingertips to extract the seeds. Be careful to protect the flesh of the grapes. Set the grapes aside in a bowl. In a preserving pan bring the collected juice to a boil, skim, and continue cooking on high heat. The syrup will be sufficiently concentrated at 221°F [105°C] on a candy thermometer. Add the muscat grapes and the apple jelly. Bring the mixture to a boil on high heat, skim, and return to a boil, cooking for about 5 minutes, stirring gently. Check the set. Put the jam into jars immediately and seal.

Muscat Grape Jam with Linden Honey

A scant 3 pounds [1.3 kg] Alsatian muscat grapes, *or* 2¼ pounds [1 kg] net
3¼ cups [700 g] sugar
3½ ounces [100 g] linden honey
Juice of 1 small lemon
⅜ teaspoon [3 pinches] ground cardamom
7 ounces [200 g] Green Apple Jelly (*page 120*)

Choose the very fragrant Ottonel muscat grapes. Rinse them in cold water and drain them by laying them on a towel. Stem them. In a bowl, combine the muscat grapes, sugar, lemon juice, honey, and cardamom and let the mixture macerate for 10 minutes. In a preserving pan bring this preparation to a simmer. Turn into a bowl, cover with a piece of parchment paper, and refrigerate overnight.

Next day, pour the mixture into a sieve, then press with the fingertips to extract the seeds. Be careful to preserve the flesh. Put the grapes aside in a bowl. In a preserving pan, bring the collected syrup to a boil, skim, and continue cooking on high heat. The syrup will concentrate sufficiently at 221°F [105°C] on a candy thermometer. Add the muscat grapes and the apple jelly. Bring to a boil once more on high heat, skim, and return to a boil for about 5 minutes, stirring gently. Check the set. Put the jam into jars immediately and seal.

Alsatian Muscat Grape Jelly

A scant 3 pounds [1.3 kg] Alsatian muscat grapes, *or* 2¼ pounds [1 kg] net
1¾ pounds [800 g] Granny Smith apples
4⅔ cups [1 kg] sugar
3⅓ cups [800 g/80 cl] water
Juice of 1 small lemon

Choose Ottonel muscat grapes. The grapes should be very fragrant. Rinse them in cold water and drain them by laying them on a towel. Stem them. Rinse the apples in cold water, core and stem them, and cut them into quarters without peeling. Put the fruit into a preserving pan and add the water. Bring the pan to a boil and let it simmer for 30 minutes on low heat. The apples will be tender. Collect the juice by pouring this preparation into a fine chinois sieve and pressing lightly on the fruit with the back of a skimmer. Then filter it a second time through cheesecloth you have soaked and wrung out. Let the juice run freely. It is preferable to let it rest overnight in the refrigerator.

Next day, measure 4¼ cups [1 kg/1 l] of the juice, leaving in the bottom of the bowl any residue that has settled out overnight. You will have clearer jelly that way. Pour the juice into a preserving pan with the sugar and lemon juice and bring it to a simmer. Skim and continue cooking on high heat for about 10 minutes, stirring gently. Check the set. Put the jelly into jars immediately and seal.

Muscat Grape Jelly with Wine

1½ pounds [650 g] Alsatian muscat grapes, *or* 1 pound 2 ounces [500 g] net
1 pound [400 g/40 cl] Granny Smith apples
1¾ cup [400 g] water
2 cups 1 ounce [500 g/50 cl] Alsatian muscat wine
4⅔ cups [1 kg] sugar
Juice of 1 small lemon

Choose the very fragrant Ottonel muscat grapes. Rinse them in cold water and drain them on a towel. Stem and core them. Rinse the apples in cold water, stem them, and cut them into quarters without peeling them. Put the fruit into a preserving pan and add the water. Bring to a boil and allow to simmer for 30 minutes on low heat. The apples will be soft. Collect the juice by pouring this preparation into a fine chinois sieve and pressing lightly on the fruit with the back of a skimmer. Filter the juice a second time by pouring it through cheesecloth you have soaked and wrung out. Let the juice run freely. It is preferable to let the juice rest in the refrigerator overnight.

Next day, measure 2 cups 1 ounce [500 g/50 cl] of the juice, leaving in the bottom of the bowl any residue that formed overnight. You will have clearer jelly that way. Pour the juice into a preserving pan with the sugar, lemon juice, and wine and bring it to a simmer. Skim and continue cooking on high heat for about 10 minutes, stirring gently. Check the set. Put the jelly into jars immediately and seal.

Vineyard Peach

2¾ pounds [1.25 kg] **vineyard peaches,** *or* **2¼ pounds** [1 kg] **net**
3¾ cups [800 g] **granulated sugar**
Juice of 1 lemon

Poach the peaches 1 minute in a pan of boiling water. Refresh them in ice water. Peel them and halve them. Remove the stones and cut each half into 6 sections.

In a preserving pan, combine the peach sections, sugar, and lemon juice. Bring to a simmer, then pour into a bowl. Cover the fruit with a sheet of parchment paper and refrigerate overnight.

Next day, bring to a boil, stirring gently. Skim. Continue cooking on high heat for about 5 minutes, stirring continuously. Return to a boil. Check the set. Put the jam into jars immediately and seal.

Vineyard Peach with Pinot Noir and Cinnamon

2¾ pounds [1.25 kg] vineyard peaches, *or* 2¼ pounds [1 kg] net

4⅔ cups [1 kg] granulated sugar

Juice of 1 small lemon

2 cinnamon sticks

1½ cups [350 g/35 cl] Pinot Noir

Poach the peaches for 1 minute in a pan of boiling water. Refresh them in ice water. Peel them and halve them, removing the stones, and cut each half into 6 sections.

In a preserving pan, combine the peach sections, sugar, cinnamon sticks, and lemon juice. Bring to a simmer, and then pour into a bowl. Cover the fruit with a sheet of parchment paper and refrigerate overnight.

Next day, bring this preparation to a boil in a preserving pan, stirring gently. Skim. Continue cooking on high heat 5 minutes, stirring constantly. Lift out the peach sections with the skimmer and divide them among the jars. Add the Pinot Noir to the cooking syrup and continue cooking on high heat for about 5 minutes. Skim again if needed. Remove the cinnamon sticks. Return to a boil. Check the set. Finish by filling the jars with the syrup and seal.

True vineyard peaches have a flavor like no other. Their delicate almond taste remains after the fruit is cooked. I advise you to select small fruit with firm flesh. Ideally, they should be picked when they're ready to fall off the tree.

By decreasing the sugar in the recipe to 1 cup, you'll have a spiced vineyard peach "soup," which you can serve very cold with a scoop of vanilla or cinnamon ice cream.

Vineyard Peach and Wild Blackberry

1½ pounds [650 g] vineyard peaches, *or* 1 pound 2 ounces [500 g] net
1 pound 2 ounces [500 g] wild blackberries
3¾ cups [800 g] sugar
Juice of 1 small lemon

Blanch the peaches for 1 minute in a pan of boiling water. Refresh them in ice water. Peel them, halve them, remove the stones, and cut each peach half into 6 sections. Pick over the blackberries and rinse them quickly in cold water without soaking them. In a preserving pan, combine the peach sections, blackberries, sugar, and lemon juice. Bring to a simmer, then pour into a bowl. Cover the fruit with a piece of parchment paper and refrigerate overnight.

Next day, bring the preparation to a boil in a preserving pan. Skim and continue cooking on high heat for 5 to 10 minutes, stirring gently. Check the set. Put the jam into jars immediately and seal.

Vineyard Peach and Raspberry with Cardamom

1½ pounds [650 g] vineyard peaches, *or* 1 pound 2 ounces [500 g] net
1 pound 2 ounces [500 g] raspberries
3¾ cups [800 g] sugar
Juice of 1 small lemon
¼ teaspoon [2 pinches] ground cardamom

Blanch the peaches for 1 minute in a pan of boiling water. Refresh them in a ice water. Peel them, halve them, remove the stones, and cut each peach half into 6 sections. Pick over the raspberries but omit rinsing them so that they'll keep their fragrance. In a preserving pan combine the peach sections, raspberries, sugar, lemon juice, and the cardamom. Bring to a simmer, and then turn into a bowl. Cover the fruit with a piece of parchment paper and refrigerate overnight.

Next day, bring the mixture to a boil in the preserving pan. Skim and continue cooking on high heat for 5 to 10 minutes, stirring gently. Check the set. Put the jam into jars immediately and seal.

Vineyard Peach and Pear with Grand Marnier

1½ pounds [650 g] vineyard peaches, *or* 1 pound 2 ounces [500 g] net

1⅓ pounds [600 g] William or Bartlett pears, *or* 1 pound 2 ounces [500 g] net

3¾ cups [800 g] sugar

Juice and finely grated zest of 1 small orange

Juice of 1 small lemon

1¾ ounces [50 g/5 cl] Grand Marnier

Blanch the vineyard peaches 1 minute in a pan of boiling water. Refresh them in ice water. Peel them, halve them, remove the pits, and cut each peach half into 6 sections. Peel the pears, halve them, core, and slice them. In a preserving pan combine the peach sections, pear slices, lemon juice, sugar, and the orange juice and zest. Bring to a simmer and turn into a bowl. Cover with a piece of parchment paper and refrigerate overnight.

Next day, bring this preparation to a boil in a preserving pan. Skim and continue cooking on high heat for 5 to 10 minutes, stirring gently. Check the set. Add the Grand Marnier liqueur. Return to a boil. Put the jam into jars immediately and seal.

Pinot Noir Jelly

---

3 cups 2 ounces [750 g/75 cl] **Pinot Noir**
1¾ pounds [750 g] **Granny Smith apples**
3 cups 2 ounces [750 g/75 cl] **water**
4⅔ cups [1 kg] **sugar**
Juice of 1 small lemon

Rinse the apples in cold water. Remove the stems and cores and cut the fruit in quarters without peeling it. Put the fruit in a preserving pan and cover it with the water. Bring the preparation to a boil and let it simmer 30 minutes on low heat. The apples will be soft.

Collect the juice by pouring the mixture into a fine chinois sieve and pressing lightly on the fruit with the back of a skimmer. Filter it a second time by pouring it through cheesecloth that you have soaked and wrung out. Let the juice run freely. It is preferable to let it rest overnight refrigerated.

Next day, measure 2 cups 1 ounce [500 g/50 cl] of the juice, leaving in the bottom of the bowl any residue that formed overnight. You will have clearer jelly this way. Pour the apple juice, wine, sugar, and lemon juice into a preserving pan and bring it to a simmer. Skim carefully and continue cooking on high heat for 10 to 15 minutes, stirring gently. Skim again if necessary. Return to a boil. Check the set. Put the jelly into jars immediately and seal.

Julienned Pear with Vanilla

2¾ pounds [1.2 kg] William or Bartlett pears, ripe but still firm,
   or 2¼ pounds [1 kg] net
3¾ cups [800 g] granulated sugar
7 ounces [200 g] Green Apple Jelly (*page 120*)
Juice of 1 small lemon
2 vanilla beans

Peel the pears, remove their stems, core them, halve them, and cut them into thin julienne. In a preserving pan, combine the pears, sugar, lemon juice, and vanilla beans, split lengthwise. Bring this to a simmer. Pour into a ceramic bowl. Cover the fruit with a piece of parchment paper and refrigerate overnight.

Next day, bring the mixture to a boil in a preserving pan. Skim. Add the apple jelly, return to a boil, and continue cooking on high heat for about 5 minutes, stirring gently. Skim again if need be. Remove the vanilla beans and divide pieces of them among the jars. Return to a boil. Check the set. Put the jam into jars immediately and seal.

Pear with Acacia Honey and Ginger

2¾ pounds [1.2 kg] William or Bartlett pears, *or* 2¼ pounds [1 kg] net

2¾ cups [600 g] granulated sugar

7 ounces [200 g] Green Apple Jelly (*page 120*)

7 ounces [200 g] acacia honey

Juice of 1 small lemon

½ teaspoon [20 g] freshly grated ginger

Peel the pears, remove their stems, cut them in two, core them, and slice them thinly. In a preserving pan, combine the pears, sugar, acacia honey, lemon juice, and grated ginger. Bring to a simmer. Pour into a bowl. Cover the fruit with a piece of parchment paper and refrigerate overnight.

Next day, bring the mixture to a boil in a preserving pan. Skim. Add the apple jelly, return to a boil and cook on high heat for about 5 minutes, stirring gently. Skim again if need be. Return to a boil. Check the set. Put the jam into jars immediately and seal.

Diced Pear with Crème de Cassis

2¾ pounds [1.2 kg] **William or Bartlett pears,** *or* **2¼ pounds** [1 kg] **net**

3 cups [650 g] **granulated sugar**

Juice of 1 small lemon

7 ounces [200 g/20 cl] **crème de cassis**

7 ounces [200 g] **Green Apple Jelly** (*page 120*)

Peel the pears, remove their stems, halve them, core them, and cut them into dice. In a preserving pan, combine the pears, sugar, and lemon juice. Bring to a simmer, and then pour into a bowl. Cover the fruit with a piece of parchment paper and refrigerate overnight.

Next day, bring the mixture to a boil in a preserving pan. Skim. Add the apple jelly and the crème de cassis. Return to a boil and cook on high heat for about 5 minutes, stirring gently. Skim again if necessary. Return to a boil. Check the set. Put the jam into jars immediately and seal.

Pear with Pinot Noir and Cinnamon

2¾ pounds [1.2 kg] ripe but still firm William or Bartlett pears,
   or 2¼ pounds [1 kg] net
4¼ cups [900 g] granulated sugar
Juice of 1 small lemon
1¼ cups [300 g/30 cl] Pinot Noir
7 ounces [200 g] Green Apple Jelly (*page 120*)
1 cinnamon stick

Select medium-sized pears. Peel them, remove the stems, halve them, core them, and cut each half into 4 wedges. In a preserving pan, combine the pears, sugar, lemon juice, and cinnamon. Bring to a simmer. Pour into a bowl. Cover the fruit with a piece of parchment paper and refrigerate overnight.

Next day, bring this mixture to a boil in a preserving pan. Skim. Add the apple jelly and pinot noir. Return to a boil and continue cooking on low heat about 15 minutes, stirring gently. Skim if necessary and return to a boil. Lift out the pears and cinnamon stick with a skimmer and divide the pears among the jars. Boil the syrup for about 5 minutes. Skim again if needed. Check the set. Finish filling the jars with the jelly and seal.

Belle-Hèléne

2¾ pounds [1.2 kg] ripe but still firm William or Bartlett pears,
   or 2¼ pounds [1 kg] net
3½ cups [750 g] granulated sugar
Juice of 1 orange
Juice of 1 small lemon
9 ounces [250 g] extra bittersweet chocolate, 68% cocoa solids*

Peel the pears, remove their stems, cut them in two, core them, and thinly slice them. In a preserving pan, combine the pears, sugar, and orange juice and lemon juice. Bring to a simmer, then pour into a bowl. Add the chocolate, grated. Mix until it is melted. Cover the fruit with a piece of parchment paper and refrigerate overnight.

   Next day, bring to a boil in a preserving pan. Skim. Continue cooking on high heat for about 5 minutes, stirring gently. Skim again if need be. Return to a boil. Check the set. Put the jam into jars immediately and seal.

* An extra-bittersweet chocolate ranked high for quality and availability is Lindt's Excellence. Excellence contains 70% cocoa, which makes it popular with professionals. Others are Callebaut, Tobler, Valrhona, and Ghirardelli. Bittersweet chocolate, called for in other jam recipes here, has 50% chocolate liquor and cocoa butter content; extra-bittersweet begins at 65% chocolate liquor.

Pear with Glacéed Chestnuts

2¾ pounds [1.2 kg] William or Bartlett pears, *or* 2¼ pounds [1 kg] net
2¾ cups [600 g] granulated sugar
¾ pounds [300 g] glacéed chestnuts
Juice of 1 small lemon
1 vanilla bean

Peel the pears, remove the stems, cut them in two, core them, and cut them into small dice. In a preserving pan, combine the pears, sugar, lemon juice, and vanilla bean, split lengthwise. Bring to a simmer and pour into a bowl. Cover the fruit with a piece of parchment paper and refrigerate overnight.

Next day, bring to a boil in a preserving pan. Skim. Add the glacéed chestnuts. Return to a boil and continue cooking on high heat for about 5 minutes, stirring gently. Skim again if need be. Remove the vanilla bean and put a piece of it in each jar. Return to a boil. Check the set. Put the jam into jars and cover.

Pear with Jasmine Mandarin Tea

2¾ pounds [1.2 kg] ripe but still firm pears, *or* 2¼ pounds [1 kg] net

4¼ cups [900 g] granulated sugar

Juice of 1 small lemon

7 ounces [200 g] Green Apple Jelly (*page 120*)

3½ tablespoons [25 g] jasmine mandarin tea

7 ounces [200 g/20 cl] water

Peel the pears, remove their stems, cut them in two, core them, and cut them into small dice. In a preserving pan, combine the pears, sugar, and the lemon juice. Bring to a simmer and then pour into a bowl. Cover with a piece of parchment paper and refrigerate overnight.

Next day, bring the preparation to a boil in a preserving pan. Skim. Add the apple jelly, return to a boil, and continue cooking on high heat for about 10 minutes, stirring gently. Skim carefully.

Meanwhile, make an infusion by pouring the hot water over the tea and letting it steep for 3 minutes.

Add the steeped tea to the jam and return to a boil. Check the set. Put the jam into jars immediately and seal.

Pear with Caramel and Spices

2¾ pounds [1.2 kg] William or Bartlett pears, *or* 2¼ pounds [1 kg] net

2¾ cups [600 g] sugar *plus* 1½ cups [300 g]

Juice of 4 oranges, *or* 7 ounces [200 g/20 cl] juice

Juice of 1 small lemon

7 ounces [200 g] Green Apple Jelly (*page 120*)

⅛ teaspoon [pinch] ground cardamom

⅛ teaspoon [pinch] ground cinnamon

⅛ teaspoon [pinch] ground star anise

Peel the pears, stem them, halve them, core them, and cut them into fine julienne. In a bowl, combine the pears, 2¾ cups [600 g] sugar, lemon juice, and spices. Cover the bowl with a piece of parchment paper and let the fruit macerate for 15 minutes. Squeeze the orange juice and heat it to lukewarm on low heat in a small saucepan. In a preserving pan, melt the sugar dry, adding a little at a time, stirring with a wooden spoon, until it is a golden caramel color. Pour the warmed orange juice into the caramel to stop the cooking. Bring it to a boil again, and then add the macerated pears. Bring the mixture to a boil and turn it into a bowl. Cover the fruit with a piece of parchment paper and refrigerate it overnight.

Next day, bring the mixture to a boil in a preserving pan. Skim, add the apple jelly, and return to a boil. Continue cooking on high heat for about 5 minutes, stirring gently. Check the set. Put the jam into jars immediately and seal.

My Grandmother's Pear Jam with Vanilla, Pine Nuts, and Walnuts

2¾ pounds [1.2 kg] ripe but still firm William or Bartlett pears,
  or 2¼ pounds [1 kg] net
3¾ cups [800 g] sugar
Juice of 1 small lemon
3½ ounces [100 g] fresh walnuts without skins
3½ ounces [100 g] pine nuts
7 ounces [200 g] Green Apple Jelly (*page 120*)
2 vanilla beans

Peel the pears, stem them, cut them in half, core them, and cut them into small dice. In a bowl, combine the diced pear, sugar, lemon juice, and vanilla beans split lengthwise. Cover the fruit with a piece of parchment paper and let it macerate for 1 hour. Turn the preparation into a preserving pan and bring to a simmer. Pour into a bowl. Cover with a piece of parchment paper and refrigerate overnight.

Next day, bring the mixture to a boil in a preserving pan, skim, add the apple jelly, and return to a boil. Continue cooking on high heat for about 5 minutes more, stirring gently. Check the set. Remove the vanilla beans, add the pine nuts and the fresh walnuts, and then return to a boil. Put the jam into jars immediately and seal.

Apple Preserves with Vanilla and Walnuts

2¾ pounds [1.2 kg] Ida Red apples,* or 2¼ pounds [1 kg] net

3¾ cups [800 g] granulated sugar

7 ounces [200 g] Green Apple Jelly (*page 120*)

Juice of 1 small lemon

1 vanilla bean

5 ounces [150 g] broken walnut meats

3 tablespoons [50 g/5 cl] water

Peel the apples, remove their stems, core them, halve them, and cut each half into 6 sections. In a preserving pan, combine the apples, sugar, water, lemon juice, and the vanilla bean, split lengthwise. Bring to a simmer. Pour into a bowl. Cover the fruit with a sheet of parchment paper and refrigerate overnight.

Next day, bring the mixture to a boil in a preserving pan. Skim. Add the apple jelly, bring to a boil, and continue cooking for 10 minutes on low heat, stirring gently. Skim carefully. Add the walnut pieces. Return to a boil. Using a skimmer, lift out the apple pieces, vanilla bean, and nuts and divide them among the jars. Boil the syrup about 5 minutes, skimming again if needed. Check the set. Finish filling the jars with the jelly and seal.

* Ida Red apples are large, bright red apples with firm, crisp, and slightly acidic white flesh.

Pear Sections with Balsamic Vinegar and Spices

2¾ pounds [1.2 kg] Passe-crassane* pears, *or* 2¼ pounds [1 kg] net

3¾ cups [800 g] sugar

3½ ounces [100 g/10 cl] balsamic vinegar

3½ ounces [100 g] floral honey

7 ounces [200 g] Green Apple Jelly (*page 120*)

1 cinnamon stick

2 star anise

4 crushed peppercorns

⅜ teaspoon ground cardamom

Peel the pears, stem them, halve them, core them, and cut each half pear into 6 wedges. In a small saucepan, bring the balsamic vinegar and honey to a boil and cook until it is reduced by half. In a bowl, combine the pear sections, sugar, spices, and vinegar with honey. Cover with a piece of parchment paper and allow to macerate overnight.

Next day, pour this mixture into a preserving pan. Bring to a simmer. Turn out into a bowl, cover with a piece of parchment paper and refrigerate overnight.

The Passe-crassane pear is the latest-ripening winter pear, short, yellow, keeps well; a cross with a quince.

On the third day, pour the mixture through a fine sieve. In the preserving pan bring the collected syrup to a boil. Skim and continue cooking on high heat. The syrup will be sufficiently concentrated at 221°F [105°C] on a candy thermometer. Add the pear sections and the apple jelly. Return to a boil on high heat. Skim, return to a boil, and boil for about 5 minutes, stirring gently. Check the set. Put the jam into jars immediately and seal.

Apple and Lemon with Cinnamon

2¾ pounds [1.2 kg] Ida Red apples,* or 2¼ pounds [1 kg] net
4 cups [850 g] granulated sugar
⅜ teaspoon finely grated lemon zest
Juice of 6 small lemons
7 ounces [200 g] Green Apple Jelly (*page* 120)
1 cinnamon stick

Peel the apples, remove their stems, core them, halve them, and slice them thinly. In a preserving pan, combine the apples, zest, lemon juice, sugar, and the cinnamon stick. Bring this mixture to a simmer and pour into a bowl. Cover the fruit with a sheet of parchment paper and refrigerate overnight.

Next day, bring this mixture to a boil in a preserving pan. Skim. Add the apple jelly, return to a boil, and continue cooking on high heat for about 10 minutes, stirring gently. Skim carefully and remove the cinnamon stick, which you will use to decorate the outside of the jars. Return to a boil. Check the set. Put the jam in jars immediately and seal.

* *Ida Red apples are large, bright red apples with firm, crisp, and slightly acidic white flesh.*

Apple with Flavors of Alsace

2¾ pounds [1.2 kg] Ida Red apples,* or 2¼ pounds [1 kg] net

3¾ cups [800 g] granulated sugar

⅜ teaspoon finely grated orange zest

Juice of 1 small orange

⅜ teaspoon finely grated lemon zest

Juice of 1 small lemon

7 ounces [200 g] Green Apple Jelly (*page 120*)

1 whole clove

2½ teaspoons [5 g] gingerbread spices†

1 rounded teaspoon [2 g] ground cinnamon

Peel the apples, remove the stems, halve them, core them, and slice them thinly. In a preserving pan, combine the apples, sugar, orange juice and zest, lemon juice and zest, and spices. Bring to a simmer and pour into a bowl. Cover the fruit with a sheet of parchment paper. Refrigerate overnight.

Next day, bring the mixture to a boil in a preserving pan. Skim. Add the apple jelly. Return to a boil and continue cooking on high heat for about 5 minutes, stirring gently. Skim carefully. Return to a boil. Check the set. Put the jam in jars immediately and seal.

---

* *Ida Red apples are large, bright red apples with firm, crisp, and slightly acidic white flesh.*
† *Épices à pain d'épices, gingerbread spice, is a blend of spices in which anise predominates, also includes cinnamon and cloves. Apple pie spice is a good substitute, with a pinch of anise.*

Apple with Lemon and Chestnut Honey

2¾ pounds [1.2 kg] apples, *or* 2¼ pounds [1 kg] net

2¾ cups [600 g] granulated sugar *plus* ½ cup [100 g]

3½ ounces [100 g/10 cl] water

7 ounces [200 g] chestnut blossom honey

1 small lemon

Juice of 1 small lemon

Rinse and scrub a lemon in cold water and slice it into very thin rounds. Peel the apples, remove the stems, halve them, core them, and cut them into small dice.

In a preserving pan, poach the lemon slices with ½ cup [100 g/10 cl] sugar, the water, and lemon juice. Cook at a boil until the slices are translucent. Add the diced apples, honey, and sugar. Bring to a simmer and pour into a bowl. Cover the fruit with a sheet of parchment paper and refrigerate overnight.

Next day, bring to a boil again in a preserving pan. Skim and continue cooking on high heat for about 5 minutes, stirring gently. Skim carefully. Return to a boil. Check the set. Put the jam into jars immediately and seal.

Apple with Caramel

2¾ pounds [1.2 kg] Ida Red apples,* *or* 2¼ pounds [1 kg] net
3 cups [650 g] granulated sugar *plus* 1½ cups [300 g]
1⅓ pounds [600 g] apples, *or* 7 ounces [200 g/20 cl] juice
Juice of 1 small lemon
7 ounces [200 g] **Green Apple Jelly** (*page* 120)

Rinse about 1⅓ pounds [600 g] apples. Remove the stems. Quarter them and put them in a juicer to extract the juice, adding the lemon juice immediately. Heat the apple juice with the lemon juice added in a nonreactive saucepan.

In a preserving pan slowly melt the sugar dry, adding it little by little and stirring with a wooden spoon, until the sugar turns the color of golden caramel. Stop the cooking by pouring in the lukewarm apple juice. Return the mixture to a boil and set aside.

Peel the remaining apples, remove their stems, halve them, core them, and cut them into julienne. Add the apples and 3 cups [650 g] sugar to the caramel and bring it to a simmer. Pour this into a bowl. Cover the fruit with a sheet of parchment paper and refrigerate overnight.

Next day, bring the mixture to a boil in a preserving pan. Skim. Add the apple jelly. Return to a boil and continue cooking on high heat for about 5 minutes, stirring gently. Skim again if need be and return to a boil. Check the set. Put the jam into jars immediately and seal.

* Ida Red apples are large, bright red apples with firm, crisp, and slightly acidic white flesh.

Apple with Julienne of Four Citrus Fruits

2¾ pounds [1.2 kg] Ida Red apples,* or 2¼ pounds [1 kg] net
3¾ cups [800 g] granulated sugar
1 grapefruit
1 orange
1 lemon
1 lime
Juice of 2 small lemons
7 ounces [200 g] Green Apple Jelly (*page 120*)

Rinse and brush the citrus fruit under cold water. Use a zester to cut long strips of zest from the four fruits and blanch the strips a few minutes in lightly salted boiling water. Refresh the zest in cool water and cut it into very narrow strips. Peel the apples, remove their stems, halve them, core them, and cut them into small dice.

In a preserving pan combine the apples, sugar, zest, and lemon juice. Bring to a simmer. Pour into a bowl. Cover the fruit with a sheet of parchment paper and refrigerate overnight.

Next day, bring the mixture to a boil in a preserving pan. Skim. Add the apple jelly. Return to a boil and continue cooking on high heat about 5 minutes, stirring gently. Skim carefully. Return to a boil. Check the set. Put the jam into jars immediately and seal.

---

* Ida Red apples are large, bright red apples with firm, crisp, and slightly acidic white flesh.

Alsace Apple and Chinese Tea

2¾ pounds [1.2 kg] apples, *or* 2¼ pounds [1 kg] net

4¼ cups [900 g] granulated sugar

Juice of 1 small lemon

7 ounces [200 g] Green Apple Jelly (*page 120*)

4½ tablespoons [30 g] Chinese tea

7 ounces [200 g/20 cl] water

Peel the apples, remove their stems, halve them, core them, and cut them in very thin slices. In a preserving pan, combine the apples, sugar, and lemon juice. Bring to a simmer, and then pour into a bowl. Cover the fruit with a sheet of parchment paper and refrigerate overnight.

Next day, bring the mixture to a boil in a preserving pan. Skim. Add the apple jelly and return to a boil. Continue cooking on high heat for about 5 minutes, stirring gently. Skim again if need be. Meanwhile, make an infusion with the water and the tea: pour the hot water over the tea and let it steep 3 minutes. Pour the steeped tea into the jam and return to a boil. Check the set. Put the jam into jars immediately and seal.

Apple and Quince Jelly with Star Anise

1¾ pounds [750 g] Ida Red apples*
1¾ pounds [750 g] apple quince or pear quince
6⅓ cups [1.5 kg/150 cl] water
5 cups [1 kg] sugar
Juice of 1 small lemon
6 star anise

Remove the slight fuzz on the quinces by rubbing them with a towel. Rinse the apples and quinces in cold water. Remove the stems and cut and core the fruit into quarters without peeling them. Put the fruit in a preserving pan and cover them with the water indicated. Bring to a boil and allow to simmer for 30 minutes on low heat. The apples and quinces will be soft. Collect the juice by pouring this preparation into a fine chinois sieve and pressing lightly on the fruit with the back of a skimmer. Filter the juice a second time through cheesecloth that you have soaked and wrung out. Let the juice run freely. It is preferable to let it rest overnight refrigerated.

Next day measure 4¼ cups [1 kg/1 l] of the juice, leaving in the bottom of the bowl the residue that settled overnight. You will have clearer jelly this way. Pour the juice into a preserving pan with the sugar, lemon juice, and the star anise and bring to a boil. Skim carefully. Continue cooking on high heat for about 10 minutes, stirring gently. Check the set, remove the star anise, and place one star anise in each jar. Return the jelly to a boil. Put it into jars immediately and seal.

* Ida Red apples are large, bright red apples with firm, crisp, and slightly acidic white flesh.

Austrian Lady

2¾ pounds [1.2 kg] Ida Red apples,* *or* 2¼ pounds [1 kg] net

3¾ cups [800 g] granulated sugar

1 vanilla bean

3½ ounces [100 g] Smyrna raisins

5 ounces [150 g] broken walnuts

Juice of 1 small lemon

1 rounded teaspoon [2 g] ground cinnamon

1¾ ounces [50 g/5 cl] rum

Peel the apples, remove the stems, halve them, core them, and cut them into thick slices. In a preserving pan, combine the apples, sugar, lemon juice, and vanilla bean, split lengthwise. In a preserving pan, bring to a simmer, and then pour into a ceramic bowl. Cover the fruit with a sheet of parchment paper and refrigerate overnight.

Next day, bring this preparation to a boil, stirring gently. Skim. Add the raisins, which have been macerated in the rum overnight, and then the cinnamon. Return to a boil and cook on high heat about 5 minutes, stirring constantly. Skim again if need be. Remove the vanilla beans, which will be used to decorate the outsides of the jars. Add the broken walnut meats. Return to a boil. Check the set. Put the jam into jars immediately and seal.

* Ida Red apples are large, bright red apples with firm, crisp, and slightly acidic white flesh.

Rowanberry* Jelly

2¼ pounds [1 kg] green apples
1¾ pounds [800 g] rowanberries
4⅔ cups [1 kg] granulated sugar
Juice of 1 small lemon
7¼ cups [1.7 kg/170 cl] water

Rinse the apples in cold water, remove the stems, core, and cut them into wedges. Strip the rowanberries from the branches and rinse them.

Put the fruit in a preserving pan and cover it with the water. Bring to a boil and let simmer on low heat for 30 minutes. The apples will be soft.

Collect the juice by pouring this preparation into a chinois sieve, pressing the fruit with the back of a skimmer. Now filter it again by pouring it through cheesecloth that has been wet and wrung out. Leave the juice in the bowl refrigerated overnight.

Next day, pour the juice (4½ cups [1.1 kg/110 cl]) into a preserving pan, being careful to leave the sediment at the bottom of the bowl in order to have clearer jelly.

Add the lemon juice and sugar. Bring to a boil and cook on high heat for about 10 minutes. Skim again if need be. Return to a boil. Check the set. Put the jelly into jars immediately and seal.

*Baies de sorbier, *sorb-tree berries, grow on the European mountain ash. Their American equivalent are rowanberries, which grow on the rowan tree. The berries are sour tasting, shiny, bright orange or red, and they appear in late summer.*

Green Tomato with Cinnamon

4 pounds [1.8 kg] green tomatoes, *or* 2½ pounds [1.1 kg] net
4⅓ cups [950 g] granulated sugar
Juice of 1 small lemon
1 cinnamon stick

Pick the last of the fall tomatoes from your garden. Select the prettiest, greenest ones. Rinse them in cold water. Dry them in a towel. Cut them in wedges and get rid of the juice, seeds, and the white center parts.

In a bowl, combine the tomato pieces, sugar, and lemon juice. Cover with a sheet of parchment paper and let macerate overnight.

Next day, pour this into a preserving pan. Add the cinnamon stick. Bring to a boil and on low heat cook 10 minutes, stirring occasionally. Pour back into a bowl. Cover with a sheet of parchment paper and again refrigerate overnight.

The third day, bring the mixture to a boil, skim, and continue cooking on low heat for 10 minutes, stirring occasionally. When the pieces are soft, put the cooked tomatoes through a food mill (fine disk), first removing the cinnamon stick, which will be used to decorate the outside of the jars.

Return the jam to a preserving pan. Return it to a boil, skim, and continue cooking on high heat for about 5 minutes, stirring constantly. Skim again if need be. Check the set. Put the jam into jars immediately and seal.

Green Tomato, Apple, and Orange

---

2 pounds [900 g] green tomatoes, *or* 1¼ pounds [550 g] net

2¼ cups [450 g] granulated sugar *plus* 2¼ cups [450 g] *plus* ½ cup [100 g]

1½ pounds [650 g] Ida Red apples,* *or* 1¼ pounds [550 g] net

Juice of 1 small lemon

1 orange

3½ ounces [100 g/10 cl] water

Pick the last of the fall tomatoes from your garden. Select the prettiest, greenest ones. Rinse them in cold water. Dry them in a towel. Cut them in wedges and get rid of the juice, seeds, and the white center parts.

In a bowl, combine the tomato pieces, 2¼ cups [450 g] sugar, and lemon juice. Cover with a sheet of parchment paper and let macerate overnight.

Next day, put this preparation into a preserving pan. Bring to a boil and continue cooking on low heat for about 10 minutes, stirring occasionally.

Pour back into a bowl. Cover with a sheet of parchment paper and refrigerate overnight.

The third day, rinse and brush the orange under cold water and slice it into very thin rounds. In a preserving pan, poach the slices with ½ cup [100 g] sugar and the water. Continue cooking at a boil until the slices are translucent. Now add the green tomato mixture. Bring to a boil, skim, and continue cooking on low heat for about 10 minutes, stirring occasionally.

Meantime, peel the apples, remove their stems, halve them, core them, and slice them thin. When the tomato pieces are soft, add the sliced apples and 2¼ cups [450 g] sugar. Bring to a boil, skim, and continue cooking on high heat for about 10 minutes, stirring gently. Skim carefully. Check the set. Put the jam into jars immediately and seal.

* Ida Red apples are large, bright red apples with firm, crisp, and slightly acidic white flesh.

Green Tomato and Pumpkin

2 pounds [900 g] green tomatoes, *or* 1¼ pounds [550 g] net
1⅓ pounds [600 g] pumpkin, *or* 1 pound 2 ounces [500 g] net
4¼ cups [900 g] granulated sugar
Juice of 3 small lemons

Pick the last of the fall tomatoes from your garden. Select the prettiest, greenest ones. Rinse them in cold water. Dry them in a towel. Cut them in segments and get rid of the juice, seeds, and the white center parts. Split the pumpkin in two, cut it into wedges, remove the seeds, peel the sections, and cut the flesh into small dice.

In a bowl, combine the tomato sections, diced pumpkin, sugar, and lemon juice. Cover with a sheet of parchment paper and allow to macerate overnight.

Next day, pour this preparation into a preserving pan. Bring to a boil, skim, and continue cooking on low heat for 10 minutes, stirring occasionally. Pour back into a bowl. Cover with a sheet of parchment paper and refrigerate overnight.

On the third day, bring the preparation to a boil in the preserving pan, skim, and continue cooking on high heat for about 10 minutes, stirring occasionally, until the tomato pieces and pumpkin dice become translucent. Skim again if need be. Return to a boil. Check the set. Put the jam into jars immediately and seal.

Ripe Tomato with Vanilla

---

4 pounds [1.8 kg] tomatoes, *or* 3½ pounds [1.1 kg] net
4¼ cups [900 g] granulated sugar
Juice of 1 small lemon
7 ounces [200 g] Green Apple Jelly (*page 120*)
2 vanilla beans

If possible, use stem tomatoes that you find in the markets toward fall. Blanch them in boiling water for 1 minute. Refresh them in ice water. Peel them, cut them into quarters, and remove the core, seeds, and excess juice. Let them drain in a colander.

In a preserving pan, combine the tomatoes, sugar, lemon juice, and vanilla beans, split lengthwise. Bring to a simmer. Pour this into a ceramic bowl. Cover with a sheet of parchment paper and refrigerate overnight.

Next day, pour the preparation into a sieve. Bring the syrup collected to a boil, skim, and continue cooking on high heat. The syrup should be sufficiently concentrated at 221°F [105°C] on a candy thermometer. Add the tomato pieces, apple jelly, and vanilla beans. Bring to a boil on high heat; skim. Return to a boil for about 5 minutes, and then remove the vanilla beans, which you will use to decorate the outside of the jars. Check the set. Put the jam in jars immediately and seal.

By reducing the sugar in this recipe to 1 cup [200 g] you will have a vanilla-flavored tomato soup, which you can serve quite cool with a scoop of vanilla ice cream and several drops of lemon-flavored olive oil.

Ripe Tomato and Apple with Rosemary

***

2¼ pounds [1 kg] ripe grape tomatoes, *or* 1 pound 2 ounces [500 g] net
1½ pounds [650 g] Ida Red apples, *or* 1 pound 2 ounces [500 g] net
3¾ cups [800 g] sugar
Juice of 1 small lemon
20 sprigs of rosemary

Select preferably the stem tomatoes that appear in the markets toward fall. Blanch them 1 minute in boiling water. Refresh them in ice water. Peel them, cut them in quarters, core them, seed them, and squeeze out their excess juice. Let them drain in a strainer. Peel the apples, cut them in two, core them, and thinly slice them.

In a preserving pan combine the tomato quarters, sliced apples, sugar, lemon juice, and the rosemary sprigs. Bring to a boil. Turn into a bowl, cover with a piece of parchment paper, and refrigerate overnight.

Next day, pour the preparation through a sieve. Bring the collected syrup to a boil, skim, and continue cooking on high heat. The syrup will be sufficiently concentrated at 221°F [105°C] on a candy thermometer. Add the tomato quarters, the sliced apples, and the rosemary sprigs. Bring to a boil again on high heat, skim, and return to a boil for about 5 minutes, stirring gently. Check the set. Put the jam in jars immediately and seal.

Gewürztraminer Wine Jelly

3 cups 2 ounces [750 g/75 cl] Gewürztraminer
1¾ pound [750 g] Granny Smith apples
3 cups 2 ounces [750 g/75 cl] water
4⅔ cups [1 kg] sugar
Juice of 1 small lemon
Finely grated zest of 1 orange

Rinse the apples in cold water. Remove the stems and cut the fruit in quarters without peeling it. Put the apples in a preserving pan and cover them with the water indicated. Bring the mixture to a boil and let it simmer for 30 minutes on low heat. The apples will be soft.

Collect the juice by pouring this preparation into a fine chinois sieve, pressing lightly on the fruit with the back of a skimmer. Filter it a second time through cheesecloth you have soaked and wrung out. Let the juice run freely. It is preferable to let it rest overnight refrigerated.

Next day, measure 2 cups 1 ounce [500 g/50 cl] of the juice, leaving in the bottom of the bowl the residue that has settled overnight. The jelly will be clearer this way. Pour the apple juice, wine, sugar, orange zest, and lemon juice into a preserving pan and bring to a simmer. Skim carefully. Continue cooking on high heat for 10 to 15 minutes, stirring gently. Skim again if necessary. Return to a boil. Check the set. Put the jelly into jars immediately and seal.

This Gewürztraminer jelly is delicious with farmstead Münster cheese.

Winter

Candied Citrus and Ginger

1¾ pounds [800 g] oranges, *or* 1 pound 2 ounces [500 g] net

1¾ pounds [800 g] grapefruit, *or* 1 pound 2 ounces [500 g] net

2 lemons

3¾ cups [800 g] sugar

11 ounces [300 g] candied ginger, diced small

Peel the oranges and grapefruit, removing all the white with the rind. Slice the fruit into rounds a little less than ½ inch [1 cm] thick. Remove the seeds and cut the slices into quarters. Rinse and brush the lemons under cold water and cut them in very thin slices. In a preserving pan, combine the citrus fruits, the sugar, and the diced preserved ginger. Bring to a simmer and turn this preparation into a bowl. Cover with a piece of parchment paper and refrigerate overnight.

Next day, pour this mixture into a preserving pan and bring to a boil, stirring gently. Skim and continue cooking on high heat for 5 to 10 minutes, stirring continuously. Check the set. Put the jam into jars immediately and seal.

~:~

Enjoy this jam with a "Fontainebleau" or fromage blanc, beaten.*

*Fontainebleau is a beaten mixture of cow's milk fromage blanc and crème fraîche, which is sold in France in plastic containers or in bulk, usually topped with a piece of mesh, plastic, or cheesecloth. Most is made in individual cheese shops.

Pineapple and Date

4½ pounds [2 kg] pineapples, *or* 2¼ pounds [1 kg] net
3¾ cups [800 g] granulated sugar
7 ounces [200 g] dates
Juice of 1 small lemon
1¾ ounces [50 g/5 cl] rum
2 vanilla beans

Slice the dates lengthwise and remove the pits. Remove the pineapples' heavy rind. Remove the eyes. Cut the pineapples into sections lengthwise. Remove the woody part of the core and thinly slice the sections.

In a preserving pan, mix the pineapple slices, sugar, dates, lemon juice, and the vanilla beans, split lengthwise. Bring to a simmer and pour into a ceramic bowl. Cover the fruit with a sheet of parchment paper and refrigerate overnight.

Next day, pour this mixture into a preserving pan and bring to a boil, stirring gently. Skim. Continue cooking on high heat for about 10 minutes, continuing to stir. Skim again if need be. Remove the vanilla beans, which you will use to decorate the sides of the jars. Return to a boil. Check the set. Add the rum. Put the jam into jars immediately and seal.

Pineapple with Vanilla and Rosemary

4½ pounds [2 kg] pineapples, *or* 2¼ pounds [1 kg] net
3¾ cups [800 g] sugar
Juice of 1 small lemon
2 vanilla beans
10 sprigs of rosemary
7 ounces [200 g] Green Apple Jelly (*page 120*)

Remove the heavy rind from the pineapples and cut them into sections lengthwise. Trim away the woody part of the core and thinly slice the sections. In a preserving pan combine the sliced pineapple, sugar, vanilla beans split lengthwise, rosemary sprigs, and lemon juice. Bring to a simmer, and then turn the mixture into a bowl. Cover it with a piece of parchment paper and refrigerate overnight.

Next day, pour the preparation into a sieve. In a preserving pan, bring the juice collected and the vanilla beans to a boil, skim, and continue cooking on high heat. The syrup will be sufficiently concentrated at 221°F [105°C] on a candy thermometer. Add the pineapple slices and the apple jelly. Bring to a boil once more on high heat, skim, and return to a boil for about 5 minutes, stirring gently. Check the set. Put the jam into jars immediately and seal.

∾:∾

You can cut the vanilla beans into little sticks and use them to decorate the outside of the jars.

Pineapple, Banana, and Coconut

1¾ pounds [800 g] pineapple, *or* 1 scant pound [400 g] net
1¾ pounds [750 g] banana, *or* 1 pound 2 ounces [500 g] net
7 ounces [200 g] fresh coconut
3¾ cups [800 g] sugar
Juice of 1 small lemon

Remove the pineapple's heavy rind, cut it into eight sections lengthwise, remove the woody part of the core, and then thinly slice the sections. Peel the bananas and cut them into round slices a little less than ¾ inch [5 mm] thick. Grate the coconut meat fine. In a preserving pan, combine the pineapple and banana pieces, the grated coconut, sugar, and lemon juice and bring to a simmer. Turn the preparation into a bowl, cover it with a piece of parchment paper, and refrigerate overnight.

Next day, pour the preparation into a preserving pan. Bring to a boil, stirring constantly, skim, and continue cooking on high heat for 5 to 10 minutes, continuing to stir. Check the set. Put the jam into jars immediately and seal.

Banana with Orange Juice and Vanilla

2¼ pounds [1 kg] bananas, *or* 1½ pounds [700 g] net

6 attractive juice oranges, *or* 1¼ cup [300 g/30 cl] juice

4 cups [850 g] granulated sugar

Juice of 1 small lemon

⅜ teaspoon finely grated orange zest

2 vanilla beans

Squeeze the oranges and reserve the juice. Peel bananas and slice them into rounds a little less than ½ inch thick. In a preserving pan, immediately combine the orange juice, banana slices, lemon juice, orange zest, sugar, and vanilla beans, split lengthwise.

Bring to a simmer. Pour into a bowl. Cover the fruit with a sheet of parchment paper and refrigerate overnight.

Next day, bring this preparation to a boil in a preserving pan, stirring continuously. Skim. Continue cooking on high heat for about 10 minutes, still stirring. Skim again if need be. Remove the vanilla beans, which will be used to decorate the jars. Mix the jam very gently. Return to a boil. Check the set. Put the jam into jars immediately and seal.

Banana with Lemon Juice

2¼ pounds [1 kg] bananas, *or* 1½ pounds [700 g] net

6 attractive lemons, *or* 7 ounces [200 g/20 cl] juice

3¾ cups [800 g] granulated sugar

⅜ teaspoon finely grated lemon zest

Squeeze the lemons. Peel the bananas and slice them into rounds a little less than ½ inch [1 cm] thick.

In a preserving pan, immediately combine the lemon juice, banana slices, sugar, and lemon zest. Bring to a simmer. Pour into a ceramic bowl. Cover the fruit with a sheet of parchment paper and refrigerate overnight.

Next day, pour this preparation into a preserving pan. Bring to a boil, stirring continuously. Skim. Continue cooking on high heat for about 10 minutes, continuing to stir. Skim again if need be. Mix the jam very gently. Return to a boil. Check the set. Put the jam into jars immediately and seal.

Banana with Bittersweet Chocolate

2¼ pounds [1 kg] bananas, *or* 1½ pounds [700 g] net

3¾ cups [800 g] granulated sugar

9 ounces [250 g] extra bittersweet chocolate, 68% cocoa solids*

7 ounces [200 g/20 cl] water

Juice of 1 small lemon

Peel the bananas and cut them into rounds a little less than ½ inch [1 cm] thick. In a preserving pan, combine the banana slices, water, sugar and lemon juice. Bring to a simmer. Pour into a ceramic bowl. Add the chocolate, grated, and mix until it is melted. Cover the fruit with a sheet of parchment paper and refrigerate overnight.

Next day, pour this preparation into a preserving pan. Bring it to a boil, stirring continuously. Skim. Mix very gently. Continue cooking on low heat for about 5 minutes, still stirring. Skim again if need be. Return to a boil. Check the set. Put the jam into jars immediately and seal.

* An extra-bittersweet chocolate ranked high for quality and availability is Lindt's Excellence. Excellence contains 70% cocoa, which makes it popular with professionals. Others are Callebaut, Tobler, Valrhona, and Ghirardelli. Bittersweet chocolate, called for in other jam recipes here, has 50% chocolate liquor and cocoa butter content; extra-bittersweet begins at 65% chocolate liquor.

Banana, Orange, and Chocolate

2¼ pounds [1 kg] bananas, *or* 1½ pounds [700 g] net
6 attractive juice oranges, *or* 1¼ cups [300 g/30 cl] juice
3½ cups [750 g] granulated sugar *plus* 1 cup [200 g]
Juice of 1 small lemon
9 ounces [250 g] extra bittersweet chocolate, 68% cocoa solids
2 attractive oranges
3½ ounces [100 g/10 cl] water

Rinse the 2 oranges under cold water and slice them into very thin rounds. Squeeze the 6 juice oranges and reserve the juice.

Peel the bananas, cut them into rounds a little less than ½ inch [1 cm] thick, and combine them with the orange juice. Mix the preparation very delicately.

In a preserving pan, poach the orange slices with 1 cup [200 g] sugar and the water. Boil until the slices are translucent. Add the banana mixture, 3¼ cups [750 g] sugar, and lemon juice. Bring to a simmer, stirring continuously. Pour into a ceramic bowl. Add the grated chocolate and mix until it is melted. Cover the fruit with a sheet of parchment paper and refrigerate overnight.

Next day, pour the preparation into a preserving pan. Bring it to a boil, stirring continuously. Skim. Continue cooking on high heat for about 10 minutes, stirring constantly. Skim again if need be. Return to a boil. Check the set. Put the jam into jars and seal.

* An extra-bittersweet chocolate ranked high for quality and availability is Lindt's Excellence. Excellence contains 70% cocoa, which makes it popular with professionals. Others are Callebaut, Tobler, Valrhona, and Ghirardelli. Bittersweet chocolate, called for in other jam recipes here, has 50% chocolate liquor and cocoa butter content; extra-bittersweet begins at 65% chocolate liquor.

Banana and Coconut

2¼ pounds [1 kg] bananas, *or* 1½ pounds [700 g] net

11 ounces [300 g] fresh coconut

3¾ cups [800 g] sugar

2 vanilla beans

4 attractive juice oranges, *or* 7 ounces [200 g/20 cl] juice

1¾ ounces [50 g/5 cl] rum

Peel the bananas and cut them into round slices a little less than ¼ inch [5 mm] thick. Break the coconut with a small hammer. The conventional way is to use a nail to poke a hole through two of the coconut's eyes, pour out the milk and strain it. Then crack the coconut wrapped in a kitchen towel by pounding it around the bottom half with a hammer. Be careful to keep the coconut milk. Remove the meat from the shell and peel away the thin skin covering it. Grate the meat fine or cut it into small, thin slices with a zester. In a preserving pan, combine the banana slices, grated coconut, sugar, orange juice, coconut milk, and vanilla beans split lengthwise. Bring to a simmer, and then turn the preparation into a bowl. Cover with a piece of parchment paper and refrigerate overnight.

Next day, pour the preparation into a preserving pan. Bring it to a boil, stirring constantly. Skim and continue cooking on high heat for 5 to 10 minutes, continuing to stir. Mix the jam carefully. Check the set. Add the rum. Return to a boil for 2 minutes. Put the jam into jars immediately and seal.

Lemon

Scant 3 pounds [1.3 kg] attractive lemons, *or* 2 cups 1 ounce [500 g/50 cl] juice

1¾ pound [750 g] Granny Smith apples

4⅔ cups [1 kg] granulated sugar *plus* 1 cup [200 g]

3 cups 2 ounces [750 g/75 cl] water *plus* 7 ounces [200 g/20 cl]

3 lemons

Rinse the apples in cold water. Remove the stems and cut the apples in quarters without peeling. Put them in a preserving pan and cover them with 3 cups 2 ounces [750 g/75 cl] water.

When the apples come to a boil, let them simmer for half an hour on low heat. The apples will be soft. Collect the juice by pouring this preparation into a fine chinois sieve, pressing lightly on the fruit with the back of a spoon. Now filter the juice a second time using cheesecloth that has been wet and wrung out, letting the juice run freely. It is best to leave this refrigerated overnight.

Next day, measure 2 cups 1 ounce [500 g/50 cl] juice, leaving in the bowl the sediment that has formed overnight, for more sparkling juice.

Squeeze the 3 pounds [1.3 kg] lemons. Measure 2 cups 1 ounce [500 g/50 cl] juice. Put the seeds in a cheesecloth bag.

Wash and brush the 3 lemons under cold water and slice them into very thin rounds. In a preserving pan, poach the lemon slices with 1 cup [200 g] sugar and 7 ounces [200 g/20 cl] water. Boil until the slices are translucent. Add the apple juice, lemon juice, 4⅔ cups [1 kg] sugar, and the seeds in the

cheesecloth bag. Bring to a boil, stirring gently. Skim. Continue cooking on high heat for about 10 minutes, still stirring. Skim again if need be. Remove the cheesecloth bag with the seeds. Return to a boil.
Check the set. Put the jam into jars immediately and seal.

∽:∼

*Ideally, this jam should be made with juice from homegrown apples, because they have more pectin. The set point is
reached faster, and the jam gains in sparkle and clarity.*

∽:∼

You can use this jam to glaze a lemon tart.

Lemon with Mountain Honey and Cinnamon

About 3⅓ pounds [1.5 kg] attractive lemons, *or* 2 cups 1 ounce [500 g/50 cl] juice

1¾ pounds [750 g] Granny Smith apples

3¾ cups [800 g] granulated sugar *plus* 1 cup [200 g]

3 cups 2 ounces [750 g/75 cl] water *plus* 7 ounces [200 g/20 cl]

7 ounces [200 g] mountain honey

3 lemons

1 cinnamon stick

Rinse the apples in cold water. Remove their stems and cut them into quarters without peeling. Put them in a preserving pan and cover them with 3 cups 2 ounces [750 g/75 cl] water.

When the apples come to a boil, simmer for half an hour on low heat. The apples will be soft. Collect the juice by pouring this preparation into a fine chinois sieve, pressing lightly on the fruit with the back of the skimmer. Now filter it a second time through cheesecloth previously wet and wrung out, letting the juice run freely. It is best to leave it overnight refrigerated.

Next day, measure 2 cups 1 ounce [500 g/50 cl] juice, leaving in the bowl the sediment that formed overnight, to have clearer jelly.

Squeeze the 3⅓ pounds [1.5 kg] lemons. Set aside 2 cups 1 ounce [500 g/50 cl] juice. Tie the seeds in a cheesecloth bag.

Wash and brush the 3 lemons under cold water and slice them into very thin rounds. In a preserving pan, poach lemon slices with 1 cup [200 g] sugar and 7 ounces [200 g/20 cl] water. Boil until the slices are translucent. Add the apple juice, lemon juice, 3¾ cups [800 g] sugar, honey, cinnamon stick, and the seeds in the cheesecloth bag. Bring to a boil, stirring gently. Skim. Continue cooking on high heat for about 10 minutes, still stirring. Skim again if need be. Remove the cheesecloth bag and the cinnamon stick, and use pieces of the cinnamon stick to decorate the sides of the jars. Return to a boil. Check the set. Put the jam into jars immediately and seal.

Lime Jelly

About 4½ pounds [2 kg] attractive limes, *or* 2 cups 1 ounce [500 g/50 cl] juice

1¾ pounds [750 g] Granny Smith apples

4⅔ cup [1 kg] granulated sugar

3 cups 2 ounces [750 g/75 cl] water *plus* 7 ounces [200 g/20 cl]

2 limes

Pinch of salt

Rinse the apples in cold water. Remove their stems and cut them into quarters without peeling. Put them into a preserving pan and cover them with 3 cups 2 ounces [750 g/75 cl] water.

Bring the mixture to a simmer and let it cook 30 minutes on low heat. The apples will be soft. Collect the juice by pouring this preparation into a fine chinois sieve, pressing lightly on the fruit with the back of the skimmer. Now filter the juice again by pouring it through cheesecloth that has been wet and wrung out, letting the juice run freely. It is best to leave it refrigerated overnight.

Next day, measure 2 cups 1 ounce [500 g/50 cl] juice, leaving in the bowl the sediment that formed overnight, to have clearer jelly.

Squeeze the 4½ pounds [2 kg] limes. Keep only the juice that remains after it has been poured through a chinois sieve. Measure 2 cups 1 ounce [500 g/50 cl]. Put the seeds into a cheesecloth bag.

Wash and brush the 2 limes under cold water, and then remove strips of zest with a zester. Poach the zest a few minutes in 7 ounces [200 g/20 cl] water and a pinch of salt.

Refresh the zest in cold water and cut it into very fine julienne.

Put into a preserving pan the apple juice, lemon juice, sugar, julienned zest, and the seeds in the cheesecloth bag. Bring to a boil, stirring gently. Skim. Continue cooking on high heat for about 10 minutes, still stirring. Skim again if need be. Remove the cheesecloth. Return to a boil. Check the set. Put the jelly in jars immediately and seal.

Clementine and Lemon with Cinnamon

2¾ pounds [1.2 kg] clementines, *or* 1¾ pounds [800 g] net

3¾ cups [800 g] sugar

2 lemons

7 ounces [200 g] Green Apple Jelly (*page 120*)

2 cinnamon sticks

½ level teaspoon ground cinnamon

Peel the clementines, taking care to remove all the white membrane. Separate them into sections and remove the seeds. Rinse and brush the lemons under cold water and slice them into very thin round slices. In a preserving pan, combine the clementines, the lemon slices, sugar, ground cinnamon, and cinnamon sticks. Bring to a simmer. Pour into a bowl, cover with parchment paper, and refrigerate overnight.

Next day, pour the preparation into a sieve. In a preserving pan bring the juice collected to a boil. Skim and continue cooking on high heat. The syrup will concentrate sufficiently at 221°F [105°C] on a candy thermometer. Add the fruit and the apple jelly and return to a boil over high heat, stirring gently. Check the set. Put the jam into jars immediately and seal.

Clementine Marmalade

1¾ pounds [800 g] **clementines**
3¼ cups [700 g] **sugar**
Juice of 2 small lemons
1¾ cups [400 g] **Green Apple Jelly** (*page 120*)

Select very thin-skinned clementines. Rinse and brush them under cold water. Cut them into very thin round slices. Remove the seeds. Cut the rounds into quarters. In a preserving pan, combine the clementine pieces, sugar, and lemon juice. Bring to a simmer. Turn into a bowl and cover with a piece of parchment paper. Refrigerate overnight.

Next day, bring the mixture to a boil again in a preserving pan, turn it into a bowl, covered with a piece of parchment paper, and refrigerate overnight.

On the third day, pour the mixture into a preserving pan. Add the apple jelly and bring to a boil, stirring gently. Skim and continue cooking on high heat 5 to 10 minutes, stirring constantly. Check the set. Put the jam into jars immediately and seal.

Christmas Jam

3¾ pounds [1.7 kg] apple-quince or pear-quince

7½ cups [1.7 kg/170 cl] water

4⅔ cups [1 kg] granulated sugar

7 ounces [200 g] dried pears, chopped fine

7 ounces [200 g] dried figs

3½ ounces [100 g] dates

3½ ounces [100 g] prunes

7 ounces [200 g] dried apricots

3½ ounces [100 g] Smyrna raisins

1¾ ounces [50 g] candied lemon rind, diced

1¾ ounces [50 g] candied orange rind, diced

1¾ ounces [50 g] preserved angelica

¼ teaspoon finely grated orange rind and juice of 1 orange

¼ teaspoon finely grated lemon rind and juice of 1 lemon

5 ounces [150 g] broken walnut meats

5 ounces [150 g] almonds, blanched and chopped

⅛ teaspoon [pinch] ground cinnamon

⅛ teaspoon [pinch] ground cardamom

⅛ teaspoon [pinch] ground star anise

1 tablespoon [5 g] anise seed

Wipe the quince with a towel to remove their slight fuzz. Rinse them in cold water, remove the stem and any remaining flower, and cut them in four. Put the quince pieces in a preserving pan and cover them with the water indicated. Bring to a boil and cook gently for an hour, stirring occasionally. Pour the mixture into a chinois sieve to collect the quince juice (5½ cups [1.3 kg/130 cl]).

Soak the chopped dried pear in this juice overnight.

Cut the figs, prunes, and apricots into julienne a little less than ¼ inch [½ cm] thick. Cut the dates in half and remove the pits. Chop the angelica fine.

Pour the macerated pears and the quince juice mixture into a preserving pan with the sugar, figs, dates, prunes, apricots, raisins, lemon peel, orange peel, angelica, orange and lemon zests, juice of the orange and lemon, and the spices. Bring to a boil, stirring constantly. Skim. Continue cooking on high heat for 5 to 10 minutes, continuing to stir. Skim again if need be. Add the walnuts and the almonds. Give the mixture a final boil for 5 minutes. Check the set. Put the jam into jars immediately and seal.

Beraweka, bread made with pears, is a tradition all over central Europe. It used to be that the bread was a delicious way to have fruit that was dried during after-harvest preparations for winter. Poire du curé, priest's pear, which is abundant in Alsace, was the variety used for this recipe. Other dried fruits were added, too, such as quetsch plums, figs, apricots, apples, preserved orange and lemon peel, and spices.

People still enjoy Beraweka today with a good glass of hot mulled wine, fragrant with cinnamon and star anise. It was in this tradition that I created the Christmas Jam.

Christmas Jelly

3 pound 5 ounces [1.5 kg] apple quince or pear quince

6⅓ cups [1.5 kg/150 cl] water *plus* 7 ounces [200 g/20 cl]

4¼ cups [900 g] granulated sugar

1 orange

Juice of 1 orange

1 lemon

Juice of 1 small lemon

⅛ teaspoon [pinch] ground cardamom

1 cinnamon stick

Pinch of salt

Wipe the quince with a towel to remove their slight fuzz. Rinse them in cold water, remove the stem and any remaining blossom, and cut them in quarters. Put the pieces into a preserving pan and cover with 6⅓ cups [1.5 kg/150 cl] water

Bring to a boil and cook for an hour on low heat, stirring occasionally. Pour into a fine chinois sieve, pressing lightly on the fruit with the back of the skimmer, and then filter the juice a second time through cheesecloth, previously wet and wrung out, letting the juice run freely. It is best to let the juice rest overnight refrigerated.

Next day, rinse and brush the orange and the lemon under cold water. Remove the zest with a zester. Cook the zest for a few minutes in 7 ounces [200 g/20 cl] boiling water with a pinch of salt. Then rinse the zest in cold water and cut it into thin sticks.

Pour the clarified quince juice (4¼ cups [1 kg/1 l] after filtering) into the preserving pan with the sugar, the zests, lemon juice, orange juice, cardamom, and cinnamon stick.

Bring to a boil, skim, and continue cooking on high heat for about 10 minutes stirring occasionally. Skim again if need be. Remove the cinnamon stick. Return to a boil. Check the set. Put the jelly into jars immediately and seal.

Kiwi and Lemon

Scant 3 pounds [1.3 kg] kiwis, *or* 2¼ pound [1 kg] net
3¾ cups [800 g] granulated sugar *plus* ½ cup [100 g]
Juice of 2 small lemons
1 lemon
3½ ounces [100 g/10 cl] water
7 ounces [200 g] Green Apple Jelly (*page 120*)

Peel the kiwis and slice them into rounds a little less than ¼ inch [5 mm] thick. Rinse and brush the lemon under cold water and slice it into very thin rounds.

In a preserving pan, poach the lemon slices with ½ cup [100 g] sugar and the water. Boil until the slices are translucent. Add the kiwis, juice of 2 lemons, and 3¾ cups [800 g] sugar.

Bring to a simmer, pour into a ceramic bowl, cover with a sheet of parchment paper, and refrigerate overnight.

Next day, pour the mixture into a preserving pan. Bring to a boil, stirring gently. Skim. Add the apple jelly, return to a boil, and continue cooking on high heat for about 10 minutes, still stirring. Skim again if need be and return to a boil. Check the set. Put the jam into jars immediately and seal.

The last indispensable
element: heat

Christmas Jam
(pages 226–27)

*Orange with Spices of
Alsace (pages 240–41)*

Pumpkin and Caramelized Lemon with a cinnamon bredala (cut-out cookie) (pages 266–67)

Pineapple with Vanilla
and Rosemary
(page 211)

Clementines and
Lemon with Cinnamon
(page 224)

Mango and Passion
Fruit (page 236)

Kumquat, Apple, and
Grapefruit Section
(page 233)

Kumquat

1¾ pounds [800 g] kumquats

3¾ cups [800 g] granulated sugar

Juice of 1 lemon

4 oranges, *or* 7 ounces [200 g/20 cl] juice

7 ounces [200 g] Green Apple Jelly (*page 120*)

Rinse and brush the kumquats under cold water. Cut them in quarters. Remove the seeds and put them in a cheesecloth bag.

In a preserving pan, combine the kumquat pieces, sugar, orange juice, lemon juice, and cheesecloth bag with the seeds. Bring to a simmer. Pour into a ceramic bowl, cover with a sheet of parchment paper, and refrigerate overnight.

Next day, return the preparation to a simmer. Pour into a ceramic bowl, cover with a sheet of parchment paper, and refrigerate overnight.

On the third day, bring to a boil in a preserving pan, stirring gently. Skim. Add the apple jelly, return to a boil, and continue cooking on high heat for about 5 minutes, stirring constantly. Skim again if need be. Remove the cheesecloth with the seeds, stirring gently. Cook for 5 minutes, continuing to stir, and skim carefully. Return to a boil. Check the set. Put the jam into jars immediately and seal.

Kumquat, Orange, and Passion Fruit

1¾ pounds [800 g] kumquats

4 oranges, *or* 7 ounces [200 g/20 cl] juice

10 passion fruit

4¼ cups [900 g] sugar

Juice of 1 small lemon

Squeeze the oranges for their juice. Rinse and scrub the kumquats with a brush under cold water. Cut them in quarters. Remove the seeds and tie them in a piece of cheesecloth. Cut the passion fruit in two, collecting the juice and the seeds. In a preserving pan, combine the kumquat quarters, the passion fruit juice and seeds, sugar, orange juice, lemon juice, and the cheesecloth containing the kumquat seeds, and bring to a simmer. Turn the mixture into a bowl, cover with a piece of parchment paper, and refrigerate overnight.

Next day, bring the mixture to a simmer again. Turn it into a bowl, cover with a piece of parchment paper, and refrigerate overnight.

On the third day, bring the mixture to a boil in a preserving pan, stirring gently. Skim and continue cooking on high heat for 5 to 10 minutes, stirring constantly. Skim again if necessary. Remove the cheesecloth with the seeds. Return to a boil. Check the set. Put the jam into jars immediately and seal.

Kumquat, Apple, and Grapefruit Section

1 pound 2 ounces [500 g] kumquats
1 pound 2 ounces [500 g] Ida Red apples,* *or* 1 scant pound [400 g] net
2 pink grapefruit
4⅔ cups [1 kg] sugar
Juice of 1 small lemon

Rinse and with a brush scrub the kumquats under cold water. Cut them in quarters and remove the seeds. Peel the apples, halve, core, and slice them. Peel the grapefruit, removing all the white membrane and cut them into round slices a little less than ½ inch [1 cm] thick. Cut the slices in quarters. In a preserving pan, combine the kumquat and grapefruit pieces, the apple slices, sugar, and lemon juice and bring to a simmer. Turn into a bowl, cover with a piece of parchment paper, and refrigerate overnight.

Next day, bring this mixture to a simmer again. Turn it into a bowl, covered with a piece of parchment paper, and refrigerate overnight.

On the third day, pour the mixture into a preserving pan. Bring to a boil, stirring gently. Skim and continue cooking on high heat 5 to 10 minutes, stirring constantly. Skim again if necessary. Check the set. Put the jam into jars immediately and seal.

* Ida Red apples are large, bright red apples with firm, crisp, and slightly acidic white flesh.

Praline Milk Jam

4¼ cups [1 kg/1 l] whole milk

6 cups [1.25 kg] sugar

9 ounces [250 g] hazelnut praline powder (*purchase at bakery*)*

9 ounces [250 g] ground blanched almonds

Pour the milk and sugar into a double boiler and cook slowly for 4 hours over very moderate heat, stirring occasionally with a wooden spoon. Be sure there is always enough water in the double boiler. The "milk jam" will develop the texture of thick honey and will be a lovely caramel blond color. Add the hazelnut praline to the milk jam and cook another hour, stirring occasionally. Add the ground almonds. Remove the jam from the double boiler. Return to a boil on high heat, stirring gently. Put the milk jam into jars immediately and seal.

Hazelnut praline powder is available through mail order sources such as King Arthur Flour and others. See Sources, page xi.

Mango

3¾ pounds [1.7 kg] mangoes, *or* 2¼ pounds [1 kg] net
3¾ cups [800 g] granulated sugar
Juice of 1 small lemon
7 ounces [200 g] **Green Apple Jelly** (*page 120*)

Peel the mangoes, remove the pits, and cut the flesh into thin slices. In a preserving pan, combine the mango slices, sugar, and lemon juice. Bring to a simmer. Pour into a ceramic bowl, cover with a sheet of parchment paper, and refrigerate overnight.

Next day, pour this mixture into a preserving pan. Bring to a boil, stirring gently; skim. Add the apple jelly. Return to a boil and continue cooking on high heat for about 10 minutes, stirring constantly. Skim again if need be. Check the set. Put the jam into jars immediately and seal.

Mango and Passion Fruit

3¾ pounds [1.7 kg] mangoes, *or* 2¼ pounds [1 kg] net
10 passion fruit
4¼ cups [900 g] sugar
Juice of 1 small lemon
7 ounces [200 g] Green Apple Jelly (*page 120*)

Peel the mangoes. Remove the flesh from the pit and cut it in small dice. Cut the passion fruit in half, collecting the juice and the seeds. In a preserving pan, combine the diced mango, juice and seeds of the passion fruit, sugar, and the lemon juice, and bring to a simmer. Pour the mixture into a bowl, cover it with a piece of parchment paper, and refrigerate it overnight.

Next day, pour this preparation into a preserving pan and bring it to a boil, stirring gently. Skim. Add the apple jelly, bring to a boil again, and continue cooking on high heat for 5 to 10 minutes, stirring constantly. Check the set. Put the jam into jars immediately and seal.

Medlar with Vanilla*

3⅓ pounds [1.5 kg] medlars, *or* 2¼ pounds [1 kg] net
3¾ cups [800 g] sugar
5 ounces [150 g/15 cl] water
2 vanilla beans

Never pick medlars before the first freeze. The medlar shell contains a delicious caramel-apple tasting pulp. Rinse the medlars in cold water and cut them in quarters. In a preserving pan bring the medlars to a boil with the water indicated, stirring with a wooden spoon. Let them boil briefly, and then put them through a food mill (fine plate).

In a preserving pan, combine the medlar pulp, sugar, and vanilla beans, split lengthwise, and bring the mixture to a boil, stirring gently. Skim if necessary and continue cooking on high heat for about 5 to 10 minutes, stirring constantly. Check the set, remove the vanilla beans, and return to a boil. Put the jam into jars immediately and seal.

∾:∾

You could also flavor this jam with a little ground cinnamon, which will be equally delicious. If you make baked apples, you can fill the core of the apples with a little of this medlar jam.

Medlars are an ancient fruit related to pear and hawthorn. The fruit, high in pectin and vitamin C, and resembling a small yellowish apple, is harvested in the fall when the leaves are falling. It is extremely tannic and "puckery," and is therefore ready to consume only after it has been "bletted," stored at room temperature for several weeks. The pulp becomes like apple butter in texture with a taste of cinnamon.

Orange Jelly with Pinot Noir and Spices

About 2¾ pounds [1.2 kg] attractive juice oranges,
  or 2 cups 1 ounce [500 g/50 cl] juice

1¾ pounds [750 g] Granny Smith apples

5½ cups [1.2 kg] granulated sugar

3 cups 2 ounces [750 g/75 cl] *plus* 7 ounces [200 g/20 cl] water

7 ounces [200 g/20 cl] Pinot Noir

2 oranges

Juice of 1 small lemon

Pinch of salt

1 cinnamon stick

⅛ teaspoon [pinch] cardamom

1 clove

Rinse the apples in cold water. Remove the stems and cut them in quarters without peeling. Put them in a preserving pan and cover them with 3 cups 2 ounces [750 g/75 cl] water.

When the apples reach a boil, simmer them for half an hour on low heat. They will be soft. Collect the juice by pouring this preparation into a fine chinois sieve, pressing lightly on the fruit with the back of the skimmer. Now filter it a second time through cheesecloth previously wet and wrung out, letting the juice run freely. It is best to leave the juice overnight refrigerated.

Next day, measure 2 cups 1 ounce [500 g/50 cl] of the juice, leaving in the bowl the sediment that formed overnight, to have clearer jelly.

Squeeze the 2¾ pounds [1.2 kg] oranges. Keep only the juice that goes through a fine chinois sieve, and set the seeds aside in a cheesecloth bag.

Wash and brush the 2 oranges under cold water, and remove the zest with a zester.

In a small saucepan, poach the zest a few minutes in 7 ounces [200 g/20 cl] water and a pinch of salt. Refresh the zest in cold water and cut it into very fine sticks.

In a preserving pan, put the apple juice, orange juice, lemon juice, sugar, julienned zest, cinnamon stick, cardamom, the clove, and the seeds in the muslin bag. Bring to a boil. Skim. Continue cooking on high heat for about 10 minutes, stirring gently. Skim again if need be. Add the pinot noir. Return to a boil and cook for about 5 minutes. Remove the cheesecloth with the seeds and remove the cinnamon stick, which you will use to decorate the sides of the jars. Return to a boil. Check the set. Put the jelly into jars immediately and seal.

Orange with Spices of Alsace

About 2¾ pounds [1.2 kg] oranges, *or* 2 cups 1 ounce [500 g/50 cl] juice and pulp

1¾ pounds [750 g] Granny Smith apples

4⅔ cups [1 kg] granulated sugar *plus* 1 cup [200 g]

3 cups 2 ounces [750 g/75 cl] water *plus* 7 ounces [200 g/20 cl]

2 oranges

Juice of 1 small lemon

2½ teaspoons [5 g] ground gingerbread spice*

1 cinnamon stick

1 star anise

Rinse the apples in cold water. Remove the stems and cut them in quarters without peeling. Put them in a preserving pan and cover with 3 cups 2 ounces [750 g/75 cl] water. Bring to a boil and let the mixture simmer for 30 minutes on low heat. The apples will be soft.

Collect the juice by pouring the apple mixture into a fine chinois sieve, pressing lightly on the fruit with the back of the skimmer. Now filter it a second time through cheesecloth previously wet and wrung out, letting the juice run freely. It is best to leave the juice refrigerated overnight.

Next day, measure 2 cups 1 ounce [500 g/50 cl] of the juice, leaving in the bowl the sediment that formed during the night, to have clearer jelly.

---

* Épices á pain d'épices, or gingerbread spice, is a blend of spices in which anise predominates, plus cinnamon and cloves. Apple pie spice may be used, with a pinch of anise.

Squeeze the 2¾ pounds [1.2 kg] oranges. Measure 2 cups 1 ounce [500 g/50 cl] juice and put the seeds into a cheesecloth bag.

Wash and brush the 2 oranges under cold water and cut them into very thin rounds. In a preserving pan poach them with 1 cup [200 g] sugar and 7 ounces [200 g/20 cl] water. Cook at a boil until the slices are translucent. Add the apple juice, orange juice, lemon juice, spices, 4⅔ cups [1 kg] sugar, and the seeds in the cheesecloth bag. Bring to a boil, stirring gently. Skim. Continue cooking on high heat for about 10 minutes, stirring constantly. Skim again if need be. Remove the cheesecloth bag of seeds and the spices. You can divide pieces of the spices among the jars. Return to a boil. Check the set. Put the jam into jars immediately and seal.

~:~

Ideally this jam should be made with juice from homegrown apples, which have more pectin. The setting point occurs more quickly, and the jelly will have more sparkle. If you have some garden apple jelly left, use it as follows: for 2 cups 1 ounce [500 g/50 cl] orange juice and pulp, use 2⅓ cups [500 g] sugar and 4 cups [900 g] jelly.

~:~

Maltese* oranges are best for this jam. You find them in the stores early in the year.

~:~

You will have a wonderful flavor combination if you fill gingerbread with a mixture of this jam and the kumquat jam.

*A good substitute for Maltese, considered to be an aristocrat among European oranges, would be a Temple, king of American oranges, or Valencia.

Blood Orange

About 2¾ pounds [1.2 kg] blood oranges, *or* 2 cups 1 ounce [500 g/50 cl] juice
1¾ pounds [750 g] Granny Smith apples
4⅔ cup [1 kg] sugar *plus* 1 cup [200 g]
3 cups 2 ounces [750 g/75 cl] water *plus* 7 ounces [200 g/20 cl]
2 oranges
Juice of 1 small lemon

Rinse the apples in cold water. Remove the stems and cut them into quarters without peeling them. Put them in a preserving pan and cover with 3 cups 2 ounces [750 g/75 cl] water.

Bring the apple mixture to a boil and simmer for 30 minutes on low heat. The apples will be soft. Collect the juice by pouring this preparation into a chinois sieve, pressing lightly on the fruit with the back of the skimmer. Filter the juice a second time by pouring it through cheesecloth previously wet and wrung out, letting the juice run freely. It is best to leave the juice overnight refrigerated.

Next day, measure 2 cups 1 ounce [500 g/50 cl] juice, leaving in the bowl the sediment that formed overnight, to have clearer jelly.

Squeeze the 2¾ pounds [1.2 kg] blood oranges. Measure 2 cups 1 ounces [500 g/50 cl] juice and put the seeds into a cheesecloth bag.

Rinse and brush the 2 oranges in cold water and slice them into very thin rounds. In a preserving pan, poach the rounds with 1 cup [200 g] sugar and 7 ounces [200 g/20 cl] water. Continue cooking at a boil until the slices are translucent.

Add the apple juice, orange juice, 4⅔ cups [1 kg] sugar, lemon juice, and seeds in the cheesecloth bag. Bring to a boil, stirring gently. Skim. Continue cooking on high heat for about 10 minutes, stirring constantly. Skim again if need be. Remove the cheesecloth with the seeds. Return to a boil. Put the jam into jars immediately and seal.

Bitter Orange*

About 4½ pounds [2 kg] bitter oranges, *or* 2 cups 1 ounce [500 g/50 cl] juice
1¾ pound [750 g] Granny Smith apples
4⅔ cups [1 kg] granulated sugar *plus* 1 cup [200 g]
3 cups 2 ounces [750 g/75 cl] water *plus* 7 ounces [200 g/20 cl]
2 oranges
Juice of 1 small lemon

Rinse the apples in cold water. Remove the stems and cut them into quarters without peeling them. Put them in a preserving pan and cover with 3 cups 2 ounces [750 g/75 cl] water.

When the apples reach a boil, simmer for half an hour on low heat. The apples will be soft. Collect the juice by pouring this preparation into a fine chinois sieve, pressing lightly on the fruit with the back of the skimmer. Now filter it a second time by pouring it through cheesecloth previously wet and wrung out, letting the juice run freely. It is best to leave the juice refrigerated overnight.

Next day, measure 2 cups 1 ounce [500 g/50 cl] of the juice, leaving in the bowl the sediment that formed during the night, to have clearer jelly.

Squeeze the 4½ pounds [2 kg] bitter oranges. Measure 2 cups 1 ounce [500 g/50 cl] juice and tie the seeds in a cheesecloth bag.

Rinse and brush the 2 oranges under cold water and slice them into very thin rounds. In a preserving

Bitter oranges are Seville-type oranges, available in some markets in late winter.

pan, poach the slices with 1 cup [200 g] sugar and 7 ounces [200 g/20 cl] water. Continue boiling until the slices are translucent.

Add the apple juice, orange juice, 4⅔ cups [1 kg] sugar, lemon juice, and the seeds in the cheesecloth. Bring to a boil, stirring gently. Skim. Continue cooking on high heat for about 10 minutes, continuing to stir. Skim again if need be. Remove the cheesecloth. Return to a boil. Check the set. Put the jam into jars immediately and seal.

Orange and Passion Fruit

About 2¾ pounds [1.2 kg] oranges, *or* 1 pound 2 ounces [500 g] orange segments
 and their juice (*about 2¼ cups*)
1¾ pounds [750 g] Granny Smith apples
5 cups [1.1 kg] granulated sugar *plus* 1 cup [200 g]
3 cups 2 ounces [750 g/75 cl] water plus 7 ounces [200 g/20 cl]
2 oranges
Juice of small lemon
10 passion fruit

Rinse the apples in cold water. Remove the stems and cut them in quarters without peeling them. Put them in a preserving pan and cover with 3 cups 2 ounces [750 g/75 cl] water. Bring the apples to a boil and simmer for half an hour on low heat. The apples will be soft.

Collect the juice by pouring this mixture through a fine chinois sieve, pressing lightly on the fruit with the back of the skimmer. Filter the juice a second time by pouring it through cheesecloth previously wet and wrung out, letting the juice run freely. It is best to let the juice remain refrigerated overnight.

Next day, measure 2 cups 1 ounce [500 g/50 cl] of the juice, leaving in the bowl the sediment that formed during the night, to have clearer juice.

Peel and section the 2¾ pounds [1.2 kg] oranges. Carefully squeeze the membrane left after sectioning the oranges in order to collect all the juice. Put the seeds in a cheesecloth bag.

Cut the passion fruit into halves. Collect the juice and seeds.

Rinse and brush the 2 oranges in cold water and slice them into very thin rounds. In a preserving pan, poach the rounds with 1 cup [200 g] sugar and 7 ounces [200 g/20 cl] water. Boil until the slices are translucent. Add the apple juice, orange juice and segments, juice and seeds of the passion fruit, lemon juice, 5 cups [1.1 kg] sugar, and seeds in the cheesecloth bag. Bring to a boil, stirring gently. Skim. Continue cooking on high heat for about 10 minutes, stirring constantly. Skim again if need be. Remove the cheesecloth bag. Return to a boil. Check the set. Put the jam into jars immediately and seal.

Coconut Vanilla

4½ pounds [2 kg] coconuts, *or* 2¼ pounds [1 kg] net

3¾ cups [800 g] sugar

7 ounces [200 g/20 cl] water

2 vanilla beans

7 ounces [200 g] **Green Apple Jelly** (*page 120*)

Break the coconut with a small hammer. Carefully collect the coconut milk. Remove the meat from the shell and use a peeler to remove the thin skin covering it. Grate the meat fine. In a preserving pan, combine the sugar, coconut milk, and water. Bring to a boil. Skim. Add the vanilla beans, split lengthwise, and continue cooking on high heat. The syrup will be sufficiently concentrated at 221°F [105°C] on a candy thermometer. Add the grated coconut and then the apple jelly. Bring the mixture to a boil again, stirring gently. Skim and continue cooking on high heat for about 5 to 10 minutes, stirring constantly. Remove the vanilla beans. Mix the jam very thoroughly. Check the set. Return the jam to a boil. Put the jam into jars immediately and seal.

Orange, Lemon, and Grapefruit with Spices

1½ pounds [650 g] Ida Red apples,* or 1 pound 2 ounces [500 g] net

2 oranges

1 lemon

1 grapefruit

4⅔ cups [1 kg] sugar

2 sticks cinnamon

¼ teaspoon ground cardamom

2 whole cloves

Rinse and scrub the citrus fruit with a brush under cold water and cut them into thin round slices. Remove the seeds and cut each round slice into quarters. Peel the apples, halve them, core them, and cut them into small dice. In a preserving pan, combine the diced apple, citrus fruit, sugar, and spices. Bring to a simmer, and then turn this mixture into a bowl. Cover with a piece of parchment paper and refrigerate overnight.

Next day, pour the preparation into a preserving pan and bring to a boil, stirring gently. Skim. Continue cooking on high heat 5 to 10 minutes, continuing to stir. Skim again if necessary. Check the set. Remove the cinnamon sticks—you'll use them to decorate the outside of the jars. Return the mixture to a boil. Put the jam into jars immediately and seal.

* Ida Red apples are large, bright red apples with firm, crisp, and slightly acidic white flesh.

Orange, Passion Fruit, and Mango

About 2¾ pounds [1.2 kg] oranges, *or* 1 pound 2 ounces [500 g] orange sections
    and juice (*about 2¼ cups*)

2 pounds [850 g] mangoes, *or* 1 pound 2 ounces [500 g] net

5 cups [1.1 kg] granulated sugar *plus* 1 cup [200 g]

7 ounces [200 g/20 cl] water

2 oranges

Juice of 1 small lemon

10 passion fruit

7 ounces [200 g] **Green Apple Jelly** (*page 120*)

Peel and pit the mangoes. Cut the mango flesh into small dice. Peel the 2¾ pounds [1.2 kg] oranges, removing all the white pith and section them, slicing into the membrane between segments to remove the sections. Carefully squeeze the remaining membrane to collect all the juice. Set the seeds aside in a cheesecloth bag.

In a preserving pan, combine the diced mango, orange sections and juice, 5 cups [1.1 kg] sugar, lemon juice, and the cheesecloth bag holding the seeds, and bring to a simmer. Pour into a ceramic bowl. Cover with a sheet of parchment paper and refrigerate overnight.

Next day, cut the passion fruits in half. Collect the juice and seeds.

Wash and brush the 2 oranges under cold water and slice them in very thin rounds. In a preserving pan, poach the orange slices with 1 cup [200 g/20 cl] sugar and the water. Cook at a boil until the rounds are translucent. Add the orange and mango mixture and the passion fruit juice and its seeds. Bring to a boil, stirring gently. Skim. Continue cooking on high heat for about 10 minutes, stirring constantly. Skim again if need be. Remove the cheesecloth with the seeds. Return to a boil. Check the set. Put the jam in jars immediately and seal.

Orange with Earl Grey Tea

About 2¾ pounds [1.2 kg] oranges, *or* 1 pound 2 ounces [500 g/50 cl] juice and
    pulp (*about 2¼ cups*)
1¾ pounds [750 g] Granny Smith apples
5 cups [1.1 kg] granulated sugar *plus* 1 cup [200 g]
3 cups 2 ounces [750 g/75 cl] water *plus* 7 ounces [200 g/20 cl]
    plus 7 ounces [200 g/20 cl]
2 oranges
4½ tablespoons [30 g] Earl Grey tea
Juice of 1 small lemon

Rinse the apples in cold water. Remove the stems and quarter them without peeling. Put them in a preserving pan and cover with 3 cups 2 ounces [750 g/75 cl] water. Bring to a boil and simmer for half an hour on low heat. The apples will be soft.

Collect the juice by pouring the mixture into a fine chinois sieve, pressing lightly on the fruit with the back of the skimmer. Now filter the juice a second time through cheesecloth previously wet and wrung out, letting the juice run freely. It is best to leave the juice overnight refrigerated.

Next day, measure 2 cups 1 ounce [500 g/50 cl] juice, leaving in the bowl the sediment that formed during the night, to have clearer jam.

Squeeze the 2¾ pounds [1.2 kg] oranges. Measure 2 cups 1 ounce [500 g/50 cl] juice and save the seeds in a cheesecloth bag.

Wash and brush the 2 oranges in cold water and slice them into very thin rounds. In a preserving pan, poach the slices with 1 cup [200 g] sugar and 7 ounces [200 g/20 cl] water.

Boil until the slices are translucent. Add the apple juice, orange juice, 5 cups [1.1 kg] sugar, lemon juice, and seeds in the cheesecloth bag. Bring to a boil, stirring gently. Continue cooking on high heat for 15 minutes, stirring constantly. Skim if need be.

Meanwhile, make an infusion with 7 ounces [200 g/20 cl] water and the tea. Allow it to steep 3 minutes. Then pour the infusion into the jam. Return to a boil, and remove the cheesecloth with the seeds. Check the set. Put the jam into jars immediately and seal.

Orange with Chocolate

About 2¾ pounds [1.2 kg] oranges, *or* 1 pound 2 ounces [500 g/50 cl] juice
  (*about 2¼ cups*)
1¾ pounds [750 g] Granny Smith apples
4⅔ cups [1 kg] granulated sugar *plus* 1 cup [200 g]
3 cups 2 ounces [750 g/75 cl] water *plus* 7 ounces [200 g/20 cl]
2 oranges
9 ounces [250 g] grated extra bittersweet chocolate, 68% cocoa solids*
Juice of 1 small lemon

Rinse the apples in cold water. Remove the stems and quarter them without peeling. Put them in a preserving pan and cover with 3 cups 2 ounces [750 g/75 cl] water.

Bring the apples to a boil and simmer for half an hour on low heat. The apples will be soft. Collect the juice by pouring it through a fine chinois sieve, pressing lightly on the fruit with the back of the skimmer. Now filter it a second time by pouring it through cheesecloth previously wet and wrung out, letting the juice run freely. It is best to leave the juice overnight refrigerated.

Next day, measure 2 cups 1 ounce [500 g/50 cl] juice, leaving in the bowl the sediment that formed overnight, to have clearer jam.

---

* An extra-bittersweet chocolate ranked high for quality and availability is Lindt's "Excellence." Excellence contains 70% cocoa, which makes it popular with professionals. Others are Callebaut, Tobler, Valrhona, and Ghirardelli. Bittersweet chocolate, called for in other jam recipes here, has 50% chocolate liquor and added cocoa butter content; extra-bittersweet begins at 65% chocolate liquor.

Squeeze the 2¾ pounds [1.2 kg] oranges. Measure 2 cups 1 ounces [500 g/50 cl] juice and save the seeds, tying them up in a muslin bag.

Wash the 2 oranges in cold water and slice them in very thin rounds. In a preserving pan, poach the slices with 1 cup [200 g] sugar and 7 ounces [200 g/20 cl] water. Boil until the slices are translucent. Add the apple juice, orange juice, 4⅔ cups [1 kg] sugar, lemon juice, and the seeds in the cheesecloth bag.

Pour this mixture into a bowl. Add the grated chocolate and mix until it is completely melted. Cover with a sheet of parchment paper and refrigerate overnight.

On the third day, bring the mixture to a boil again, stirring gently. Continue cooking on high heat for about 10 minutes, stirring constantly. Skim again if need be. Remove the cheesecloth bag with the seeds. Return to a boil. Check the set. Put the jam into jars immediately and seal.

Orange and Angelica with Orange Blossom Honey

About 2¾ pounds [1.2 kg] oranges, *or* 1 pound 2 ounces [500 g/50 cl] juice
  (*about 2¼ cups*)
1¾ pounds [750 g] Granny Smith apples
4 cups [850 g] granulated sugar *plus* 1 cup [200 g]
3 cups 1 ounce [750 g/75 cl] water *plus* 7 ounces [200 g/20 cl]
7 ounces [200 g] orange blossom honey
3½ ounces [100 g] preserved angelica stem
2 oranges
Juice of 1 small lemon

Rinse the apples in cold water. Stem and quarter them without peeling. Put them in a preserving pan and cover them with 3 cups 2 ounces [750 g/75 cl] water. When the apples come to a boil, simmer for half an hour on low heat. The apples will be soft.

Collect the juice by pouring it through a fine chinois sieve, pressing the fruit lightly with the back of the skimmer. Now filter it a second time by pouring it through cheesecloth previously wet and wrung out, letting the juice run freely. It is best to leave the juice refrigerated overnight.

Next day, measure 2 cups 1 ounce [500 g/50 cl] juice, leaving in the bowl the sediment that formed during the night, to have clearer jam.

Squeeze the 2¾ pounds [1.2 kg] oranges. Measure 2 cups 1 ounces [500 g/50 cl] juice and keep the seeds, tying them up in a cheesecloth bag.

Wash and brush the 2 oranges under cold water and slice them in very thin rounds. Rinse the angelica stems to remove the syrup on them and cut them into sticks a little less than ½ inch [1 cm] wide.

In a preserving pan, poach the orange rounds with 1 cup [200 g] sugar and 7 ounces [200 g/20 cl] water. Continue boiling until the slices are translucent. Add the apple juice, orange juice, 4 cups [850 g] sugar, honey, lemon juice, angelica sticks, and the seeds in the cheesecloth bag. Bring to a boil, stirring gently. Skim. Continue cooking on high heat for about 10 minutes, stirring constantly. Skim again if need be. Remove the cheesecloth with the seeds. Return to a boil. Check the set. Put the jam into jars immediately and seal.

In the spring, you can make this jam with fresh angelica. If so, add ½ cup [100 g] sugar to the recipe.

Orange and Kumquat Jelly with Cinnamon

2¾ pounds [1.2 kg] oranges, *or* 2 cups 1 ounce [500 g/50 cl] juice

9 ounces [250 g] kumquats

1 pound 2 ounces [500 g] Granny Smith apples

3 cups 2 ounces [750 g/75 cl] water

4⅔ cups [1 kg] sugar

Juice of 1 small lemon

2 cinnamon sticks

Rinse and scrub the kumquats with a brush under cold water, and then rinse the apples. Cut the kumquats and apples into quarters. Put them into a preserving pan and cover them with the water indicated. Bring to a boil and let the mixture simmer for 30 minutes on low heat. The apples will be soft.

Collect the juice by pouring the mixture into a fine chinois sieve, pressing lightly on the fruit with the back of a skimmer. Filter it a second time by pouring it through cheesecloth, which you have soaked and wrung out. It is preferable to let the juice rest overnight in the refrigerator.

Next day, measure 2 cups 1 ounce [500 g/50 cl] of the juice obtained, leaving in the bowl the residue that formed overnight. You will have clearer jelly this way.

Squeeze the 2¾ pounds [1.2 kg] oranges and measure 2 cups 1 ounce [500 g/50 cl] juice. Pour the apple and kumquat juice, orange juice, sugar, lemon juice, and cinnamon into a preserving pan and bring it to a simmer. Skim and continue cooking on high heat for about 10 minutes, stirring gently. Skim if necessary. Check the set. Remove the cinnamon sticks. Return to a boil. Put the jelly into jars immediately and seal.

Grapefruit and Honey

3½ pounds [1.6 kg] pink grapefruit, *or* 2¼ pounds [1 kg] net

3¾ cups [800 g] sugar

3½ ounces [100 g] mountain honey

Juice of 1 small lemon

7 ounces [200 g] **Green Apple Jelly** (*page 120*)

Rinse and scrub the grapefruit with a brush under cold water. Remove the zest from two grapefruits with a zester and cut it into narrow slivers. Remove the rind and white pith and then slice the grapefruit into round slices a little less than ¼ inch [5 mm] thick. Remove the seeds and cut the rounds into quarters.

In a preserving pan, combine the grapefruit pieces, sugar, honey, and slivered zest. Bring to a simmer, and then turn the mixture into a bowl. Cover with a piece of parchment paper and refrigerate overnight.

Next day, pour the mixture into a fine sieve. In a preserving pan, bring the syrup collected to a boil, skim, and continue cooking on high heat. The syrup will be sufficiently concentrated at 221°F [105°C] on a candy thermometer. Add the grapefruit pieces with the zest and the apple jelly. Bring to a boil again on high heat, stirring gently. Skim and return to a boil for about 5 minutes, stirring constantly. Check the set. Put the jam into jars immediately and seal.

~:~

This jam is delicious with a barely sweetened vanilla crème brûlée.

Pink Grapefruit Jelly

About 2¼ pounds [1 kg] pink grapefruits, *or* 2 cups 1 ounce [500 g/50 cl] juice
1¾ pounds [750 g] Granny Smith apples
3 cups 2 ounces [750 g/75 cl] water *plus* 7 ounces [200 g/20 cl]
4⅔ cups [1 kg] granulated sugar
1 pink grapefruit
Juice of 1 lemon
Pinch of salt

Rinse the apples in cold water. Remove the stems and quarter the apples without peeling them. Put them in a preserving pan and cover with 3 cups 2 ounces [750 g/75 cl] water. Bring the apples to a boil and simmer for half an hour on low heat. The apples will be soft.

Collect the juice by pouring it through a fine chinois sieve, pressing the fruit lightly with the back of the skimmer. Now filter it a second time through cheesecloth previously wet and wrung out, letting the juice run freely. It is best to leave the juice refrigerated overnight.

Next day, measure 2 cups 1 ounce [500 g/50 cl] juice, leaving in the bowl the sediment that formed during the night, to have clearer jam.

Squeeze the 2¼ pounds [1 kg] pink grapefruit. Keep only the juice that goes through the chinois sieve. Set aside the seeds, tied in a cheesecloth bag.

Wash and use a brush to scrub the 1 pink grapefruit under cold water, and remove strips of zest with a zester. In a small saucepan, poach the grapefruit zest with 7 ounces [200 g/20 cl] water and a pinch of salt. Refresh the zest in cold water and cut it into very thin julienne.

Put in a preserving pan the apple juice, grapefruit juice, 4⅔ cups [1 kg] sugar, lemon juice, julienned zest, and the seeds in the cheesecloth bag. Bring to a boil, stirring gently. Skim. Continue cooking on high heat for about 10 minutes, stirring constantly. Skim again if need be. Remove the cheesecloth bag with the seeds. Return to a boil. Check the set. Put the jam in jars immediately and seal.

Pear and Medlar*

1⅓ pounds [600 g] Passe-crassane pears, *or* 1 pound 2 ounces [500 g] net
1¾ pounds [750 g] medlars, *or* 1 pound 2 ounces [500 g] net
3½ ounces [100 g/10 cl] water
3¾ cups [800 g] granulated sugar
Juice of 1 small lemon

Never pick medlars before the first frost. It's then that the pulp inside the fruit's shell has the taste of caramelized apple. Rinse the medlars in cold water and cut them in quarters. In a preserving pan, bring the medlars to a boil with the water, stirring with a wooden spoon. Let the mixture boil for a few minutes, and then put it through a food mill (fine disk).

Peel the pears, halve them, core them, and cut them into thin slices. In a preserving pan combine the medlar pulp, pear slices, sugar, and lemon juice. Bring the mixture to a boil, stirring gently. Skim and continue cooking on high heat for about 10 minutes, stirring constantly. Check the set. Put the jam into jars immediately and seal.

*Medlars are ancient fruit related to pear and hawthorn. The fruit, high in pectin and vitamin C, and resembling a small yellowish apple, is harvested in the fall when the leaves are falling. It is extremely tannic and "puckery," and is therefore ready to consume only after it has been "bletted," stored at room temperature for several weeks. The pulp becomes like apple butter in texture with a taste of cinnamon.

Pumpkin with Vanilla

A scant 3 pounds [1.1 kg] pumpkin, *or* 2¼ pounds [700 g] net

4 oranges, *or* [200 g/20 cl] of juice

4¼ cups [900 g] granulated sugar

3½ ounces [100 g/10 cl] water

2 vanilla beans

Juice of 1 lemon

Split the pumpkin in half and cut it into 8 sections. Remove the seeds, peel the sections, and cut the flesh into fine julienne. In a ceramic bowl, combine the pumpkin, sugar, lemon juice, orange juice, water, and vanilla beans split lengthwise. Cover with a sheet of parchment paper and let macerate overnight.

Next day, pour into a preserving pan and bring to a simmer. Pour back into a bowl. Cover with a sheet of parchment paper and refrigerate once more overnight.

On the third day, bring this preparation to a boil in the preserving pan, stirring gently. Skim. Continue cooking on high heat for 10 to 15 minutes, continuing to stir. Skim again if need be. Remove the vanilla beans, which you will divide among the jars. Return to a boil. Check the set. Put the jam into jars immediately and seal.

Pumpkin with Wine and Spices

2¼ pounds [1 kg] pumpkin, *or* 1⅓ pounds [600 g] net

3¾ cups [800 g] sugar

1¾ cups [400 g/40 cl] Gewürztraminer

Juice of 1 small lemon

⅜ teaspoon ground cinnamon

⅜ teaspoon ground cardamom

⅜ teaspoon ground nutmeg

7 ounces [200 g] Green Apple Jelly (*page 120*)

Split the pumpkin in half and cut it into 8 wedges. Remove the seeds, peel the sections, and cut the flesh into very small dice. In a preserving pan, combine the pumpkin, sugar, wine, lemon juice, and spices. Bring to a simmer and pour into a bowl. Cover with a piece of parchment paper and refrigerate overnight.

Next day, pour this mixture into a preserving pan, add the apple jelly, and bring to a simmer, stirring gently. Skim and continue cooking on high heat for 5 to 10 minutes, stirring constantly. Mix the jam very thoroughly. Return it to a boil. Check the set. Put the jam into jars immediately and seal.

Pumpkin with Dried Apricots and Citrus

1¼ pounds [550 g] pumpkin, *or* 13 ounces [350 g] net

11 ounces [300 g] dried apricots

2¾ cups [600 g] sugar

1 pound 1 ounce [450 g] oranges

1 lemon

7 ounces [200 g/20 cl] Gewürztraminer

Cut the dried apricots into sticks a little less than ¼ inch [5 mm] thick and macerate them in a bowl with the Gewürztraminer. Split the pumpkin and cut it into sections. Remove the seeds, peel the sections, and cut the flesh into very small dice. Rinse and brush the citrus fruit under cold water. Cut them into very thin round slices. Remove the seeds and cut each round into quarters.

In a preserving pan, combine the macerated apricots, the diced pumpkin, the citrus pieces, and sugar. Bring to a simmer and turn this preparation into a bowl. Cover with a piece of parchment paper and refrigerate overnight.

Next day, pour the preparation in to a preserving pan. Bring to a boil, stirring gently, skim, and continue cooking on high heat for about 10 minutes, stirring constantly. Skim again if necessary. Check the set. Put the jam into jars immediately and seal.

Pumpkin and Caramelized Lemon

2½ pounds [1.1 kg] pumpkin, *or* 1½ pounds [700 g] net

3¾ cups [800 g] granulated sugar *plus* 1 cup [200 g]

3½ ounces [100 g/10 cl] water

8 lemons, *or* 8½ ounces [250 g/25 cl] lemon juice

2 attractive lemons

1¾ ounces [50 g] acacia flower honey

Split the pumpkin in half and cut it into 8 sections. Remove the seeds, peel the sections, and cut the flesh into very small dice. In a ceramic bowl, combine the pumpkin, 3¾ cups [800 g] sugar, juice from 8 lemons, and honey. Cover with a sheet of parchment paper and let macerate overnight.

Next day, pour this into a preserving pan and bring to a simmer. Pour back into the bowl. Cover with a sheet of parchment paper and refrigerate overnight.

On the third day, rinse and brush the 2 lemons in cold water and slice them into thin rounds. In a preserving pan, poach the rounds with 1 cup [200 g] sugar and the water. Continue cooking until the slices are translucent and the syrup begins to caramelize lightly. Take the pan off the heat. With a fork, lift out the caramelized slices and put them on a piece of parchment paper. Pour the pumpkin preparation into the preserving pan that still contains a little caramelized sugar. Bring the mixture to a boil, stirring gently. Skim. Continue cooking on high heat for about 15 minutes, continuing to stir. Skim again if need be. Return to a boil. Check the set. Slip the lemon slices into the jars so that they stand on their rims against the insides of the jars (3 slices per jar). Put the jam into the jars and seal.

~:~

For caramelizing the lemon slices, which are going be the decorative accent in the jars, it's helpful to have a wide preserving pan with a flat bottom. The slices will lie flat side by side. They will keep their shape better and will cook at the same rate, all becoming candied and reaching the right point of caramelization at the same time.

Index

J

Fig jam with Vanilla, 163

Greengage Plum jam with Vanilla and Dried Lemon
    Slices, 135

Julienned Pear jam with Vanilla, 180

Medlar jam with Vanilla, 237

Mirabelle Plum jam with Gewürztraminer and
    Vanilla, 98

My Grandmother's Pear Jam with Vanilla, Pine
    Nuts, and Walnuts, 188

Nectarine and Pear jam with Vanilla, 66

Pineapple jam with Vanilla and Rosemary, 211

Pumpkin jam with Vanilla, 263

Ripe Tomato jam with Vanilla, 204

Rose Hip jam with Vanilla, 161

Two Kinds of Apricots with Vanilla and
    Gewürztraminer, 60–61

Vineyard peach jams:

Vineyard Peach, 173

Vineyard Peach and Pear with Grand Marnier, 178

Vineyard Peach with Pinot Noir and Cinnamon,
    174–175

Vineyard Peach and Raspberry with Cardamom, 177

Vineyard Peach and Wild Blackberry, 105, 176

Violets:

Raspberry jam with Essence of Violet, 75

W

Walnuts:

Alsatian Quetsch Plum and Dried Quetsch Plum
    jam with Walnuts, 129

Apple Preserves with Vanilla and Walnuts, 189

in Austrian Lady jam, 199

Chestnut and Fresh Walnut jam, 146

in Christmas Jam, 226–227

Dried Fruit and Apple Slice jam with Fresh
    Walnuts, 142–143

in Dried Fruit and Honey jam, 141

Fig, Orange, and Walnut jam, 164

Green Melon jam with Lemon and Walnuts, 95

My Grandmother's Pear Jam with Vanilla, Pine
    Nuts, and Walnuts, 188

Spiced Green Walnut jam, 33

Watermelon, Apple, and Grapefruit jam, 111

White cherry jams:

White Cherry with Raspberry, 13

White Cherry à la Rose, 14

White peach jams:

Raspberry and White Peach, 74

White Peaches with Saffron, 116

White Peach with Lemon Verbena, 117

White Peach with Rose de Chine Tea, 115

Yellow and White Peach, 114

Wild Apple Jelly with Cinnamon and Citrus Zest, 126–127

Wild blackberries:

A Trio of Wild Berries, 104

Old Bachelor's Jam with Wild Blackberries, Raspberries, and Kirsch (variation), 112–113

Wild Blackberry jam, 102

Wild Blackberry Jelly, 106

Wild Blackberry and Vineyard Peach jam, 105, 176

Wild Blackberry and Wild Raspberry jam, 103

Wild blueberries:

A Trio of Wild Berries, 104

Old Bachelor's Jam with Wild Blueberries, Raspberries, and Kirsch, 112–113

Wild Blueberry jam, 64, 107

Wild Blueberry jam with Pinot Noir and Licorice, 108

Wild Blueberry and Lemon jam, 109

See also Blueberries

Wild Prune and Green Apple Jelly, 123

Wild raspberries:

A Trio of Wild Berries, 104

Wild Blackberry and Wild Raspberry jam, 103

Wild strawberries:

Strawberry jam with Elderberry Blossoms, 32

Wild Mara Strawberry and Wild Strawberry jam, 25

Wine:

Muscat Grape Jelly with Wine, 172

Pumpkin jam with Wine and Spices, 264

See also Gewürztraminer; Pinot noir

Y

Yellow Peach jam with Lavender Honey, 118

Yellow Peach and Orange jam, 119

Yellow and White Peach jam, 114

Z

Zucchini and Pepper jam with Spices, 71